# Performance Guide for Electronic Keyboard and Organ

## Grade 1 to Diploma

**by**

# Andy Smith and Tony Pegler

To enter for an examination, or for more details and syllabuses, please contact:

LCM Examinations
Thames Valley University
Walpole House
18-22 Bond Street
London W5 5AA

tel: +44 (0)20 8231 2364
fax: +44 (0)20 8231 2433

email: lcm.exams@tvu.ac.uk
http://mercury.tvu.ac.uk/lcmexams

or your local representative

Published by:

LCM Publications
Thames Valley University
Walpole House
18-22 Bond Street
Ealing
London W5 5AA

ISBN: 0 9528375 4 4

By Andy Smith and Tony Pegler

# Contents

# About the Authors

Andy Smith and Tony Pegler are two well-respected musicians who between them have over 50 years of experience in music education, instrument development and performance. They have always shared a passion for the development and creative use of the electronic organ and keyboard, and have a long held belief that everyone should be assisted to enjoy their own musical output at any musical level.

This book offers their insight to the often overcomplicated world of orchestration and arranging, using the modern technology available on the electronic organ and keyboard of today.

**Andy Smith GLCM LTCL LLCM(TD)** is a graduate of the London College of Music where he studied piano, organ and orchestral conducting. After further study in Sienna, and with Sir Adrian Boult, Andy found that his love of conducting and arranging for an orchestra could be satisfied in a new way – the electronic organ – a whole orchestra at your fingertips.

This talent was further utilised in his work for various electronic musical instrument manufacturers, performing in concerts and music festivals worldwide. Andy later became the manager of Technics Music Academy where he helped develop the nationwide schools, which boasted over 7000 students.

Andy is now an examiner for LCM Examinations as well as keeping a very busy schedule as a professional musician, composer, arranger and music copyist.

© Simon Gill

**Tony Pegler FLCM** has a reputation within the organ and keyboard fraternity which makes him a sought-after performer by industry manufacturers. His specialist knowledge is evident in the accompaniment styles that he has written for various instruments.

As a concert artist and demonstrator for Thomas, Lowrey, Technics and currently Yamaha, Tony has performed around the world as well as extensively in the UK.

He has also made several CDs and instruction videos and regularly contributes editorials and teaching articles to music magazines. Tony has taught in many of the UK's leading colleges and universities, which have produced some of today's leading organists. Tony continues to work in all of these fields as well as the very live situation of a theatre pit orchestra. He has recently become an examiner for LCM Examinations.

# Introduction

The modern electronic keyboard and organ are imitative instruments and are designed to be used as such. The purpose of this book is to equip anyone interested in creating orchestrally realistic performances with a basic understanding of the instruments' features and effects and how to incorporate them into a prepared arrangement. Accepting that purchasers of these instruments are of all ages and ability, the information contained in the following pages is for everyone and not for the exclusive use of the more advanced player. Most of this book has been written to embrace even the most modest talent.

As a practical guide this book will lead you through;

- how the setup of an orchestra, band or ensemble is relevant to the sounds you will find on your instrument;

- how to arrange a song in your favourite style;

- understanding how chords work and the importance of chord inversions;

- how to improvise;

- how to create your own rhythm and accompaniment patterns;

- how to prepare and record a sequence;

- how to use creative features such as Auto-melodic Harmony and Registration Memories;

- how best to use your instrument's sounds, and know that you are playing them in a realistic note range.

Whether you are studying on your own or with a teacher, playing for leisure or preparing for an exam, the information contained in this book will be invaluable to those striving to improve not only their playing, but also their understanding and use of their instrument. You will make mistakes – certainly, you will press the wrong button – inevitably, but only a few times. Knowing why, is the first step to understanding how, and with today's modern instruments, you are only limited by your imagination.

Throughout the book, music examples highlight and support the text. The enclosed CD contains audio recordings of all examples to illustrate aurally what you are learning. By working through the book you should be able to discover how to reproduce these on your own instrument.

*NB: References to examination requirements contained in this book are for guidance only. Candidates and teachers should consult the current syllabus for further information.*

# 1. ORCHESTRATION

This chapter will help you to get the best sound from your instrument and ensure that your performances are as musically realistic as possible. But before we learn the art of orchestration, it is important that you know a little about 'sampling', the technology behind your instrument's sounds.

## What is sampling?

Most electronic keyboards and organs available today produce sounds using a technology known as sampling. This technology (PCM – Pulse Code Modulation), originally invented by the telecommunications industry, has been developed over the last 30 years by various manufacturers. During this time, sampling has become the universal way of capturing sounds for use on both keyboards and organs.

Before sampling, sounds were created with the use of analogue technology which used electronic circuitry to recreate the individual waveforms of each sound. The result was acceptable in its day, but always lacked that natural realism. Sampling is far more realistic because it is a digital recording of the instrument being played live by a professional musician. This recording is then manipulated and edited, so that when you play the sound, you are essentially listening to a CD quality recording of that actual instrument. Some manufacturers have made this sampling technology even more realistic by capturing not only the sound of an instrument, but also its harmonic structure as well – e.g. piano samples with acoustic resonance and hammer noise.

## What is orchestration?

Orchestration is the art of blending sounds, just as an artist uses a variety of coloured paints to bring his or her drawing to life. The availability of fabulous realistic sounds has not made playing the keyboard or organ any easier; in a way it has made it more difficult, as you now need a fundamental knowledge of all these instruments in order for your performances to be realistic and therefore more musical.

Samuel Adler in his book *The Study of Orchestration* states that

> Since so many musicians deal with the great instrument we call the orchestra,
> it is important that the study of orchestration and instrumentation becomes a
> basic part of every musician's education.  (W. W. Norton & Co., 2002)

Therefore the study of orchestration and instrumentation is especially important for keyboard players and organists using today's instruments. Having this fundamental knowledge will ensure that you have the understanding and skill to create realistic and musical performances at any grade, using the fantastic sounds which are now available.

The fundamental knowledge required is:

- The range of the individual instruments and their characteristics
- How they perform as a solo instrument
- How they perform within an ensemble

Chapter 7: Instruments and Suggested Listening has details on all of these for a wide range of commonly used orchestral and band instruments.

There are many excellent books on the subject of orchestration, including, for a classical approach:

> *Treatise on Instrumentation* by Hector Berlioz (Music Sales, 1991)
>
> *Orchestration* by Walter Piston (W. W. Norton & Co., 1955)
>
> *Orchestration* by Cecil Forsyth (Dover, 1982)

and for a more contemporary approach:

*Sounds and Scores* by Henry Mancini (Music Sales, 1997)

*The Contemporary Arranger* by Don Sebesky (Alfred Music Co., 1975)

*The Complete Arranger* by Sammy Nestico (Fenwood Music, 2005)

These are all excellent books and well worth reading; however, the detailed knowledge and application which they contain are aimed at the composer and orchestrator, rather than the electronic keyboard player and organist. With that in mind, this chapter (and also chapter 7) will endeavour to translate that vast knowledge and explain in simpler terms how it can be applied to your instrument.

The art of orchestration is a very personal one. Each composer, arranger, keyboard player or organist can create a totally different sound using the same instruments. In this respect it is the same as harmony, melody or in fact any other musical parameter, but in order to personalise your sound, it's imperative that you understand the basic skills of orchestration to start with.

There are no definitive rights or wrongs; it is purely a matter of what is musical and realistic – therefore it is good practice for you to listen to all kinds of musical genres, so that you can then form your own opinions and tastes.

To help with this, there is a suggested listening list at the end of the book (see Chapter 7: Instruments and Suggested Listening). This is by no means definitive, and is merely a starting point to help you to expand your musical awareness... Listen to everything and anything.

## Understanding the sounds

Generally, we can organise the sounds on your instrument into two main categories – Ensemble and Solo.

- **Ensemble** sounds emulate the sound of a number of instruments all playing together to create one particular sound. A good example of this would be the string section or the brass section of an orchestra.

- **Solo** sounds emulate the sound a solo instrument. You can of course, keyboard or organ permitting, combine three or four solo sounds to create your own ensemble.

Before looking at the ensemble sounds and how they are best used, we need to be aware of what the different sections are, and which individual instruments combine to make each section. Generally, with the exception of the rhythm section, each section can be likened to a vocal choir, as they each have a Soprano, Alto, Tenor and Bass voice.

Solo instruments can also be split into two groups, depending on their polyphony. Woodwind and brass instruments are monophonic, which means they can only generate one note at a time, whereas the strings, guitars and pianos are polyphonic, which means they can generate more than one note at a time. However, although the solo strings are polyphonic, this kind of polyphony (double stopping) is used sparingly.

Understanding all this will be of assistance when creating your own ensemble combinations.

# What now?

## How do you start orchestrating?

Orchestration is a very skilled art. In a real life situation, a composer or arranger, especially in the theatre, film and TV industry, will employ an orchestrator to orchestrate their music – such is the skill of the professional orchestrator. So you can see just how important it is to understand all the available sounds, and put them together so that they sound musical and realistic.

So where do you begin? Firstly you need to have arranged the piece of music you wish to orchestrate (see Chapter 2: Arranging) as this will give you an idea of the style and of course the length of the piece. As stated before, there are no definitive rights or wrongs to orchestration, but there are some fundamental principles which should be adhered to. For example, it would not be realistic or musical to play a piece all the way through using a woodwind or brass sound, as in reality, the player would be gasping for breath, and the listener's attention would also start to fade.

## Melody lines

Think carefully about your choice of orchestration for melody lines, and ask yourself a few questions:

- Are my choices suited to the musical genre?
- Am I playing the instrument within its range?
- Is it possible for the real instrument to play this, and for this length of time?

When you have chosen your sound, think about how a live musician would play the melody. If you choose piano, think pianistically, making good use of touch sensitivity, if your instrument has the facility. If you choose a woodwind or brass sound, allow the virtual player to breathe, by phrasing the melody. Giving your arrangement shape and colour in this way will not only make the piece more musical and realistic, but it will also help maintain the listener's complete attention.

## Accompaniment

The accompaniment also needs the same care and attention. First, it must be carefully balanced with the melody line, ensuring it is not too overpowering and that it is in keeping with the musical genre that you are trying to create. Do not use *String Ensemble* or *Organ* throughout, as again this can become monotonous.

As an idea for a slow ballad, maybe after the intro, the melody could be introduced, accompanied by simple arpeggios on a *Nylon Guitar* or *Modern EP*. The sustained chords of the *String Ensemble* could then be introduced second time round or at the chorus. This will not only give the arrangement good musical shape, but it will also keep the listener's attention, as the arrangement is musically interesting and surprising. Be it an examination or concert performance, this detailed attention to orchestration is vitally important.

Listen carefully to as many different musical genres as possible, and take notice of the way professional orchestrators and arrangers use the various instruments. Focus on the recording and try to note down which sounds are being used.

Orchestrators and arrangers specialise in different musical genres, so it is important to know who the orchestrator/arranger is when listening, so that you can become aware of each orchestrator/arranger's style. For example Johnny Mandel and Claus Ogerman are supreme string arrangers, while David Foster and Vince Mendoza offer great examples of how to treat a popular music standard with a lush orchestration. These are just four fine examples; there are of course many other fine orchestrators and arrangers.

Finally, remember that the orchestration suggestions in the LCM graded handbooks are just that – suggestions. Use your imagination and understanding of the many sounds available to you to create your own realistic musical arrangements.

# 2. ARRANGING

You may not be aware of it, but you are subjected to the arranger's art every time you hear a piece of music being played on the radio, TV, CD or at a live concert. It does not matter about the style, instruments or notes because it's the arranger's job to decide who plays what, when and how. To create your arrangement there are various musical tools you can use. The grade and standard of musicianship will dictate which are the most suitable.

## Musical form

So what is musical form and why is it so important? A good musical arrangement, like a good piece of music, should have structure or form. The fundamental musical forms include **A**, **AB** (binary), and **ABA** (ternary), and there are other more complex forms such as sonata form.

**A** form is one section of music or a repeated chord progression, often referred to in popular music as simple verse form. A good example of this is a 12 bar blues.

The most common form in popular music is a variation on **ABA** or **AABA** with **A** representing the verse and **B** the chorus. The **A** section usually ends on the tonic, then a modulation to the dominant key (which is common for the **B** section) prepares us for the return of the final **A** section, in the tonic. A good example of this form is 'I Got Rhythm' by George Gershwin

In later popular songs a compound version of **AABA** has been used, where a contrasting bridge section separates two 32 bar sections (**AABA – Bridge – AABA**) A good example of this is 'Every Breath You Take' by The Police.

It is vital when arranging that you remember these fundamental forms, as an arrangement without structure can be unsettling for the listener – like a journey without any direction.

Once you have identified the form/structure of a piece you can illustrate it with your choice of registrations and auto accompaniments. Each section should use a different combination of sounds, with the auto accompaniment building from the start, to an 'all bells and whistles' ending. This is why each auto accompaniment on your instrument will have at least four variations.

To create a simple arrangement using these fundamental forms is quite easy; in fact if you analyse the pieces within the LCM graded handbooks you will see that all of them use one or other of these fundamental forms. For more in-depth information on musical form, see the following:

*Musical Form and Musical Performance* by E. T. Cone (W. W. Norton & Co., 1968)
*Forms of Music* by Donald Francis Tovey (OUP, 1957)
*American Popular Song* by Alec Wilder (OUP, 1972)
*Studying Popular Music* by Richard Middleton (OUP, 1990)

## Three basic features

Another essential tool is an in-depth knowledge of your instrument's features and how they work. Getting to know all of your instrument's features can take time, and learning about these features should form part of any lesson from Grade 1 upwards, but there are three basic features which even a beginner should be capable of using, and they are:

- Panel Memory or Registration Memory
- Fills or Fill-ins
- Intros and Endings

It used to be that each manufacturer would have required a separate chapter regarding the use of these features, and that switching from one brand to another was a whole new learning curve. Today, however, although the various manufacturers' instruments sound slightly different, most brands share a basic set of features that are no longer unique.

## Panel Memory or Registration Memory

Changing registrations while playing can be quite difficult, but there are two features which can be used to aid a smooth musical change. Storing your registrations into 'Panel Memory' / 'Registration Memory' is paramount for a quick and musical registration change. It is often impossible to push various buttons, alter volume sliders, etc. and still maintain a smooth musical change. Used in conjunction with a foot-switch, panel memory makes the change even smoother, as your hands do not have to leave the keyboard.

Most mid-price and above instruments will have this facility, and it is probably one of the most useful features on your instrument. These memory buttons will usually store not only right and left hand registrations, but also auto accompaniment settings and parameters such as variation selection, tempo, the volume settings of each of the individual accompaniment parts, and which accompaniment parts are on or off. You can also store transposition information and your split point settings as well as effects settings for reverb and chorus. (Check your owner's manual for the exact parameters that can be stored.)

Using just three registrations, with three auto accompaniment variations, each with sound, volume and other parameter changes, will enable you to present a musical performance. The creative skill is in choosing your three registrations.

Once you have stored all this data, you should save it on whatever storage media your instrument has – normally it is a 3.5" floppy disk. This saves time when preparing your piece for a live performance, be it in a concert or during your examination.

## Fills or Fill-ins

If you analyse the musical form of your piece in depth, you will find that each section, within most popular songs, is usually organised in four or eight bar (measure) phrases with a major break at the end of sixteen bars. This break will be a musical or rhythmic phrase that will either ease the flow of one section into the next, or will bring one section to a close and then lead you on to the next. This major break is often referred to as a 'fill' or 'fill-in' and usually lasts for just one bar. Sometimes the drummer will play a roll round the kit, or maybe the guitarist will play a rhythmic figure (riff) or maybe the entire band will be playing a musical figure based on the dominant seventh chord which leads to the next section.

If you are not sure what a fill-in should sound like, just set an accompaniment playing, press the 'Fill' or 'Fill-in' button and listen. Another option would be listening to recordings of different styles of popular music, and in particularly the last bar of a phrase. You will hear a fill-in of some kind.

Try and identify 'soft' fills which link the half-way point in the same section together (bars 4-5 or 8-9) and the 'hard' fill which leads into the chorus or middle eight/bridge section.

Like the rhythmic qualities of a melody, fills add motion to a piece and they can certainly add to its dynamics; let the piece dictate where you use them. As a general rule, trigger the fill-in during the bar before the start of the next phrase.

On most instruments, a fill lasts for just one bar and if you press the 'Fill' button either on the beat or just before the bar in which you want your fill to play, you'll hear the complete bar's fill-in pattern. The fill will automatically stop at the end of the bar, at which point, the normal style variation will cut back in again. In 4/4, if you press the fill on beat three then you'll get a half bar fill – which is very handy if you are playing a slow piece, as a whole bar fill-in would just be too long. If you start the fill on beat four, you will probably get the last beat of the fill plus the whole of the next bar too. In 'Playground' (on page 13), try a half bar fill in bars 4 and 8 and a four beat fill at bars 12 and 16.

Some mid to high range instruments have fills that are dedicated to each accompaniment variation and certain brands have fills that are musically designed to lead into the next variation, so it's worth taking a close look at just how your instrument's fill system works. Fills are a very useful arranger's feature as they add realism to your finished work and will make your arrangements much more musically structured.

Introducing fill-ins is just as difficult as changing registration, so if your instrument has the facility, assign a foot-switch to engage the fill as and when you want it.


## Intros and endings

Whenever possible, but certainly from Grade 3 upwards, an arrangement should have an intro and ending, as this will create the right mood for your piece before the main melody begins and brings it to a musically structured conclusion with an ending. From Grade 5 upwards these should be based on the piece being performed as opposed to simply using the in-built intros and endings found on most electronic keyboards and organs.

Intro is short for introduction, which is a musical device used to establish the general style of the piece. It can be just a few pick-up beats from the drummer, or a full-blown orchestrated eight bar 'scene setter'. However, not all pieces have or need an intro. For instance, Glenn Miller's 'Moonlight Serenade' doesn't, nor does Procol Harum's 'A Whiter Shade of Pale' or the Beatles' 'Hey Jude'. On the other hand with some pieces the intros are so well known that you can't really perform the piece without it: 'In The Mood' for example, The Carpenters' 'Close To You' or John Lennon's 'Imagine'.

To use an in-built intro, you'll need to establish the key in which the piece you are about to play is written, as your instrument needs this information in order to play its intro in the correct key.

Another useful feature when starting a performance is 'Synchro start'. This feature means that as soon as you play your first chord, either with or without the intro, the auto accompaniment will start. This is a much more professional way to start your performance, and it is certainly easier than trying to play a chord, press 'Start', and play a melody note simultaneously.

Generally, you should use the intro or ending that goes with the selected accompaniment. However, if your instrument has a large selection of accompaniment styles, you may find that the intro from another style would be better suited for your arrangement. If this is the case, it will be a musical choice that you have made and is a perfect example of using your instrument's features musically and creatively to make your arrangements realistic.

Another very effective way to use an existing intro or ending is to play along with it. Pick the part that you would most like to play and write the notes down so that you always have a record of it – it is easy to remember while you are working on a piece, but not quite so easy six months later. This is certainly a much more musically satisfying way of playing an in-built intro or ending than just letting your instrument do it.

An ending obviously needs to happen at the end of your piece, and again, you can either use the one that is dedicated to the accompaniment which you are using, or you could use the ending from a different accompaniment if you think it better suits your arrangement. The ending needs to begin from the downbeat of the bar once the score has finished; but quite often, the ending needs to begin at the last note of the melody.

As with the intro, your ending is a self-contained composition in the style of your chosen auto accompaniment, complete with its own melody and chord changes. When using an in-built ending, so that it works musically, you will need to play the basic tonic triad in the key of the last section of your piece and press the ending button of your choice (if there is a choice). As with changing registrations and fill-ins, this can be tricky, so, if your instrument has the facility, use a foot-switch to do it. Again this helps the performance to flow smoothly and musically.

These three features, plus all the other features and effects, are tools that, when used creatively, can help you to produce an effective and creative arrangement of even the simplest of pieces.

As a guide, these are the features with which we recommend you should be familiar at the various graded levels:

For **Grades 1-3** you should ideally be familiar with:

- all of your instrument's individual sounds and how to locate them;
- how to mix sounds together and balance the volume of one sound against another;
- how to add an effect to a sound, such as chorus or repeat;
- how to store your registrations (sometimes referred to as 'Panel Memories' or 'Registration Memories');
- how to save your registrations to disk or some other storage media;
- how to reload the stored registrations from disk or internal memory;
- all of your instrument's rhythm patterns, auto accompaniments and variations;
- how to turn off, where possible, specific instruments within the auto accompaniment;
- the feature that turns a single right hand melody note into a chord (depending on the manufacturer, this feature is known as 'Techni-chord', 'Harmony', 'Auto-Harmonise' or 'Melody on Chord') see Chapter 6: Auto-melodic Harmony;
- how to sequence a simple step-time control track (see Chapter 3: Sequencing).

For **Grades 4 and 5** we recommend that you increase your knowledge to include:

- panning, if your instrument permits: a feature which allows you to place sounds within the stereo image (see Chapter 3: Sequencing);
- how to re-voice the default chord and bass sound: a feature that plays your chord when the auto accompaniment is turned on, but not playing;
- the different harmony styles available from your right hand chord feature, and how to assign them to a particular sound, if your instrument permits.

For **Grades 6 and 7** you should also be familiar with:

- how to use the 'multi-track sequencer' to create a basic sequence to enhance your live performance (see Chapter 3: Sequencing);
- the ability to play in a pianistic style with auto accompaniment in 'Full Keyboard Mode' (keyboard players only);
- how to create your own auto accompaniment patterns, often known as the 'Composer' or 'Style Creator' feature;
- basic sound editing – changing the parameters of a sound to make it unique ('pitch shift', 'attack, decay & release time', 'vibrato rate, depth & delay').

For **Grade 8** and onwards, every single feature on your instrument should be fully understood, and utilised musically and creatively.

This is quite an extensive list, and it will take some time for you to become completely familiar with all of these features. However, as you discover how creative each of these features is, it will become apparent how best to use it.

## Starting a basic arrangement (Grades 1-3)

An arrangement can be as simple as you want to make it, and the old adage 'less is more' is one that any arranger should keep in mind. The more sounds you mix together, the less of each individual one you will hear. The same applies with notes too – it is easier to hear four notes than it is to hear ten, and just by changing the sounds, you can completely alter the mood of a piece. As an example, here is an extract from the LCM Grade 1 Handbook (LL172/LL180) called 'Playground':

### Example 1

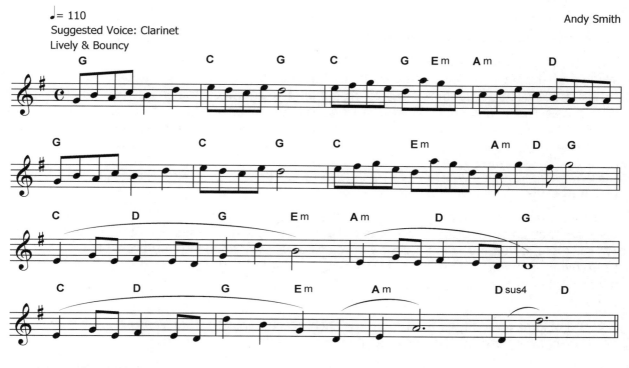

This melody line and chord symbol arrangement is often referred to as a 'lead sheet', 'top line and chords' or even a 'busker's version' and is a general outline for the piece. Unlike a fully notated score, a 'lead sheet' conveys the required harmony in an abbreviated form, i.e. chord symbols, which are a condensed form of all of the notes (harmony) that support the melody. There is no written rhythm for the harmony, so it is therefore a musical decision for you to make as to how the melody's accompaniment should be performed. This gives you a musical freedom which a fully written arrangement cannot, and you can therefore decide the style, chord inversions and general feel of the piece, irrespective of what the composer suggests.

'Playground' was conceived as a piece in a lively and bouncy 16-beat style, suggesting that you should perform it using any one of the 16-beat auto accompaniments available on your instrument, at a tempo of 110 bpm (beats per minute), using a clarinet sound for the tune.

To begin arranging this piece, play it through a couple of times and familiarise yourself with how it sounds with the suggested registration and then try the following examples of how the piece's character can be easily changed:

## 1. Play the melody using a different sound.

Whatever you choose will make you respond differently when you play the keys. A flute sound will make the keys feel 'spongy' and you will automatically want to play in a smooth legato manner with longer phrases, whereas a guitar sound will make the keys feel spiky and percussive, and you will play in a more detached way.

## 2. Change the tempo.

A 16-beat at 110 bpm is quite fast and most definitely 'lively'. Slowed down to around 80 bpm, this same rhythm will sound more like a modern pop ballad. The important thing here is that you will sense that the piece is more gentle and melodic and this will inevitably change the way you perform it. Remember, however, that any such change of tempo should be made for clear musical reasons, and not simply to make the piece easier to play!

## 3. Change the auto accompaniment.

The 'Playground' melody is written with straight quavers (eighth notes), therefore you must avoid swing and shuffle styles because they have a quaver 'triplet' feel. Try a Rock & Roll style and then a Latin style such as Beguine; just by responding to the accompaniment you will play the piece with a new feel – and that's more than enough to give it a new lease of life. You can play the same piece with any of the auto accompaniments available on your instrument and it will seem like a new piece every time.

## Musical style

Another item in the arranger's toolkit is musical style. Having tried the above example, you will discover that each auto accompaniment requires a right hand melody sound that suits the style. For example, if you are using a gentle Bossa Nova accompaniment, you probably wouldn't play the tune using a banjo, as they rarely appear in Latin bands and ensembles. Likewise, if your accompaniment is a heavy metal band then you would not use that pretty orchestral flute for the melody.

You will also have changed the tempo for each accompaniment that you try. That is because each accompaniment pattern has a unique style and therefore a suitable tempo.

A style is a recognised assortment of sounds that amalgamate to produce a particular rhythm and feel, which is then used by the musical world in general when there is a need to duplicate that experience. Before you start, deciding on the style of your arrangement is vitally important, as it makes the process of arranging a piece so much easier.

The Beatles, Glenn Miller, Mantovani, Drum & Bass, Hip Hop, Jazz, Northern Soul, even a Tom & Jerry cartoon or a piece of Sci-Fi music all have characteristics that are unique; a sound such that when you hear it, you instantly know what the piece is and who is playing it. Glenn Miller sounds like Glenn Miller, whether the band is playing 'Moonlight Serenade' or 'Moon River'. If you want to play a song in the style of Mantovani, then you probably won't be looking for your brass sounds. The Beatles' classic, 'Hey Jude', only sounds acceptable at a certain tempo; play it too fast or slow and it simply sounds wrong. Over time, these styles and their respective melody sounds have become standard musical fare and as such, the various manufacturers have devoted much time and effort to creating auto accompaniments that accurately reflect a particular musical style.

Whatever style you choose, remember that the phrasing and choice of sounds is vital in order to create a musical arrangement. Simply playing the tune 'as written' to a Drum & Bass rhythm may not work musically, and as a result you may lose marks for a lack of musical integrity.

## 'Playground' arrangement

Now that you have gained some tools to create your first basic arrangement, here is an example and analysis of how you can make a basic arrangement very effective.

On the analysis you can see the following:

- The original markings have been removed or changed because this is now an arrangement of the piece, rather than an 'as written' performance;
- The tempo is now slower and the auto accompaniment style is an 8-beat rather than the double feel of a 16-beat;
- The extra four bars at the beginning contain a melodic line taken from an 'in-built' intro and is there as a guide only;
- Notice also that the intro is from a different auto accompaniment style to the first part of the piece;
- The Em chord in bar 7 has been replaced with G and Em for harmonic interest.

**Example 2**

# PLAYGROUND

Andy Smith

So that you do not get two intro melody lines, mute the part in the auto accompaniment style that contains this copied line, so that the only one you hear is the one that you play. This 'muting' forms part of your first 'panel memory' or 'registration memory' together with the sound that you want to use, which can be either the same sound as the original accompaniment part, or something else that you feel is appropriate – another musically creative decision for you to make. The other panel / registration memory set-ups are really a matter of choice; use sounds that are associated with the accompaniment you are using and if you are unsure what they are, listen to some recordings of in a similar style, or simply test them out.

The chosen intro uses a dreamy string sound, which needs to fade gradually after the last note, rather than coming to an abrupt halt. To ensure this happens you will see that there is an instruction to turn 'Sustain' on just before the note is to be released and off again at the end of the bar. You could do this with a foot-switch of course, but if you don't have one or are unsure about its use, then programming this data using a 'control' track will ensure that you achieve the right result (see Chapter 3: Sequencing).

The use of fills is a matter of personal taste. You will notice that there are quite a few here, but you can see that they either cover a long note or come at the end of a phrase. Don't forget that this version of the piece is much slower than the original, which means that the notes actually last longer and the phrases will seem longer too, so there is much more space in the piece for these extra fills. Also, there is an accompaniment style variation so that you can pick up a different fill in bars 16 and 20.

The second section of the piece (from bar 13) changes accompaniment style, but still retains the same feel to it; it has a new registration too – your choice – and although the registration does not change, you will see that 'harmony' (right hand chords from a single note) is activated at bar 17. You could press the button yourself, but it is easier to use the control track.

The last phrase also has a different registration, which should be selected and stored in Registration Memory 4. For this to work successfully, you will need to create a quaver rest at the beginning of beat four in bar 18. This makes a space for the registration memory change to actually take place. This also means changing the last note in bar 18 to a quaver, so don't be afraid of changing things a little to accommodate your personal touches; after all, this is only what happens in reality.

This is only part of 'Playground', but the same basic procedure will take you through to the end of the piece, including finding an ending that fits, and maybe transcribing one of the melodic lines in the auto ending, so that you can play along. This kind of basic arrangement is more than acceptable as an approach for Grade 1 through to Grade 3. However, as you progress through the grades, your musicianship should also advance, and your pieces might start to include harmonic embellishments such as chord substitutions, chord extensions and modulations.


## Harmony and chord structure (Grades 4-8)

Playing an electronic keyboard or organ requires an in-depth musical knowledge which other instrumentalists do not necessarily need in order to perform. One such piece of knowledge is an understanding of harmony and chord structures. A comprehensive knowledge of this nature, from Grade 1 through to Grade 8, can be gained from the LCM/Registry Publications Popular Music Theory books. The corresponding examination syllabus is also worth considering.

When you play a keyboard-based instrument, any notes you play in addition to the melody are harmony; whether it is a second single line producing just one additional note or every finger simultaneously playing a note each – it is all harmony.

## Understanding the basics

Before you begin to understand harmony and chord structures, you need not only to know, but also to fully understand your scales, at whichever grade. Scales not only provide assistance with your fingering technique and dexterity, but also give you an insight into the relationship between the various keys and how a piece is structured harmonically. The next section, although aimed principally at Grade 4 upwards, should be interesting for all levels; however you must understand a little, if not all, of the following:

- How major and minor scales are constructed;

- How the blues, pentatonic and modal scales are constructed;

- How each note of the scale relates to the others;

- The importance of the dominant note (the fifth note of the scale), and the leading note (the seventh note of the scale);

- Intervals;

- That a basic triad consists of the tonic note, the third and fifth notes of the scale, and that this represents intervals of a major third and a minor third in the case of a major chord, and a minor third and major third for a minor chord;

- The different chord inversions such as root, first inversion and second inversion;

- Chord extensions such as 6ths, 7ths, 9ths, 11ths and 13ths.

If any of the above is totally alien to you, then ask your teacher to explain, or refer to the Popular Music Theory books mentioned above.

There are many chords to learn and understand, together with their characteristics, and how best to use them. However, the way you use these chords will be determined by the kind of instrument that you play. For example, an organ has pedals for the bass, whereas on a piano, you have to use the keys in the lower register; a keyboard adds an automatic bass note, computed from a chord played to the left of a split point.

Therefore, each instrument is not only played differently, but the mental approach is different too. In general, a pianist will usually 'see' a chord as including a bass note, whereas an organist 'sees' a chord as two separate parts – a pedal note and the keyboard notes. The keyboard player is not always aware of the relevance of the tonic – the root note of a chord – but, like the organist, will probably have a better understanding of chord inversions than the piano player. Whatever your instrument, understanding how harmony and chords work is vitally important.

Chords and their construction make for a fascinating subject; they have the power to create every kind of emotion, and can change it in an instant. On one hand it is sometimes the case that the harmonic foundation upon which the melody sits can have a greater power to control mood and movement than the melody itself. However, on the other hand, in some pieces when the melody is heard on its own, it will convey, of its own accord, the harmony which it requires ('implied harmony'). Which begs the question – which came first, the melody or the harmonic structure?

In the early grades, you will be using basic triad chords, like C, F and G, but when using your instrument's auto accompaniments, you may well hear added harmony notes. This is because the manufacturer has created stylised accompaniments using the harmonic characteristics of a particular musical style, and interprets the physical chord that you play.

For instance, a Big Band swing style will use 6th and 9th chords in the accompaniment, even if you only play the basic major triad. A Pop Ballad will probably use 2nds, added 9ths and a few 'suspensions', again, even if you only play a basic major chord.

## Auto-melodic harmony

The same applies to the 'harmony' feature on your instrument as well. Although different manufacturers will give the style of these harmonies their own descriptive names, you will almost certainly have Close Harmony, Open Harmony, Duet (two parts), Trio (three parts), Block Harmony, Jazz Open Harmony and Jazz Closed Harmony, etc. If you use this feature but don't really know how or why it works, then understanding harmony and chord structures will most certainly help. It will also assist you to achieve the best results from your instrument's harmonic feature, as well as enabling you to construct an arrangement of your own, at any level. For more knowledge on this harmony feature read Chapter 6: Auto-melodic Harmony.

The ability to read both written musical notation and chord symbols is a great advantage, and both have their merits. While in popular music, it is more common for pianists to read a fully notated score, organ and keyboard players tend to use a combination of both written notation and chord symbols. Chord symbols are merely a musical shorthand way of writing a fully notated chord.

## Chord inversions

The chord symbol has the advantage of being a much more flexible medium when notating how you want the harmony (the notes in the supporting chord) to sound. Change a chord's inversion and you change its sound – and when it comes to arranging (as well as choosing the sounds that you are going to use) the chord inversion is important, as the top note of the chord has a special relationship to the melody.

Try the following example and listen to how certain chord inversions sound better with the melody.

### Example 3

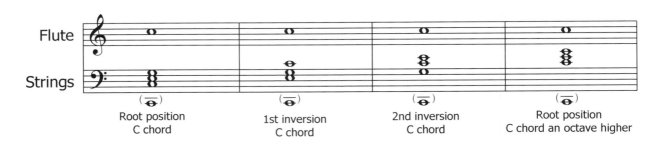

Root position
C chord

1st inversion
C chord

2nd inversion
C chord

Root position
C chord an octave higher

*Check that the bass clef notes are sounded at normal (concert) pitch.*

*It is usual when auto accompaniment is selected on a keyboard that the notes to the right of your split point will probably sound an octave lower, and the notes to the left of your split point, will sound an octave higher. The pitch of some solo instruments may automatically change on a keyboard or organ to reflect the range in which the instrument is pitched in reality. (See Chapter 7: Instruments and Suggested Listening). If you are playing an organ, use sounds pitched at 8'.*

*NB: To hear auto bass, turn on the auto accompaniment section but do not press 'Start'. Keyboard players should play the bass clef notes an octave lower. The notes in brackets are the bass notes which are added automatically via the auto accompaniment or played on the pedals.*

While the C melody note sounds adequate with all of the chord inversions, you will probably find that the second inversion sounds the most pleasing. The reason for this is that the interval between the C melody note and the top note of this particular inversion is a sixth. From C down to the E below is six notes in the C major scale, and intervals of a sixth or a third – its octave counterpart – sound very harmonious and easy on the ear. Use your aural skills to detect this.

A different melody note will also have a chord inversion with which it sounds best:

**Example 4**

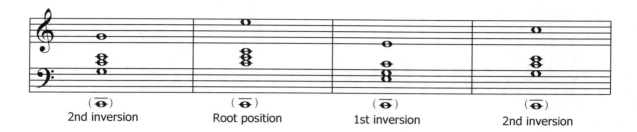

| 2nd inversion | Root position | 1st inversion | 2nd inversion |

Expand this idea further to take into account the chord changes that happen in a piece, and you should start to see that there is enormous potential for some simple, but most effective, non-rhythmic arranging.

Try this out using the first four bars of 'Playground'. Play it through a few times without using particular chord inversions, with the same flute and string registrations as before.

**Example 5**

*NB:. This includes the additional G chord in bar 3 (as in Example 2).*

Now try it with the chord inversions given in this example, where the melody note is enhanced by the chord's highest note:

**Example 6**

*NB: Rt = Root position, 1 = 1st inversion, 2 = 2nd inversion, 3 = 3rd inversion.*

You will hear that the top note of the chord is now quite melodic in its own right. In the following example it is transcribed for the right hand and written in the treble clef.

**Example 7**

## Adding chords – substitutions

'Playground' is a simple piece, but can be made more musically interesting by adding extra chords or 'substitutions'. For example, if you play the first bar of Example 5, you might sense that a different chord should be played for the two notes on the second beat.

The 'trick' with all chord 'substitutions' is to know your destination: the overall harmony for bar 1 is G (major) and if you add a chord at beat two, it needs to be a chord that leads you to the next one. The type of chord which does this is called a 'dominant seventh'. You might not know this type of chord by name, but you will certainly recognise it – it's the penultimate chord in this well-known phrase:

**Example 8**

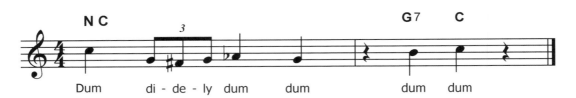

Dum    di - de - ly dum    dum       dum    dum

Try stopping on that G7 chord in bar 2 – it's almost impossible; you just have to play that final chord. The dominant 7th chord has the power to lead, and it is this effect that you need to create harmonic movement to the next chord.

In 'Playground', add a seventh chord at beat two in bar 1, and it will lead you back to the G chord – your destination – at beat three. Similarly, in bar 2, the notes that make up the second beat will also benefit from an additional chord, both from a harmonic and rhythmic point of view. The same principle applies; and although this bar starts with a C chord, any chord that you add at beat two has to lead to the destination chord of G.

**Example 9** *(Note the added D7 chords)*

20

## Circle of fifths

Knowing which dominant 7th chord to use is easy, once you understand the most important harmonic tool available to us – 'the circle of fifths', so called because each key is a 5th away from its neighbour.

This is what it looks like...

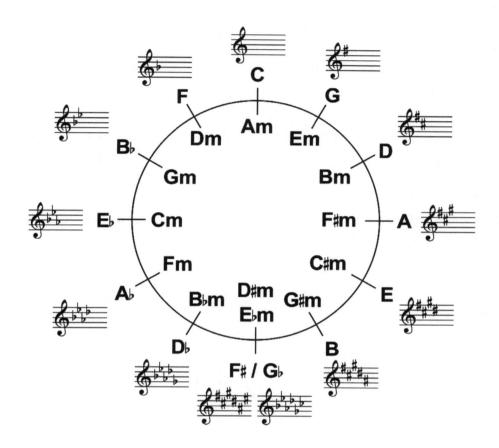

...and this is how it works:

By adding a 7th to any chord, it will lead you to the next anti-clockwise chord in the circle. This 7th chord is known as a dominant 7th, and its tonic is the fifth note or dominant note of the chord you are moving to.

For example, if your destination is Bb, you can get there via F7; if you want to get to D, go via A7 and so on. This also works if your destination is a minor chord; G7 will lead to Cm and E7 to Am; you will also find that this works if your starting chord is minor too, so, Gm7 to Cm and Em7 to Am.

A dominant 7th chord adds the flattened seventh note of its tonic scale to the tonic chord. For instance, a C7 chord uses the tonic triad of C major (C, E, G) plus the flattened seventh note which is a Bb.

There is one other basic seventh chord and that is the major seventh. This chord adds the seventh note of the major scale to the tonic triad. So a Cmaj7 chord is C, E, G and B.

Applying this simple procedure to the 'Playground' piece makes it easy to see which chords you could use. See Example 10 on page 22.

**Example 10**

There are a few points to look at here:

- You could have added a G7 chord at bar 1 beat four, but if you want the change to the C chord at the beginning of bar 2 to be more noticeable, this would not work as well.

- In bar 3 the D7 sounds better with the E melody note than it does with the preceding G melody note.

- Also in bar 3, you could have added an Em7 chord on the last quaver to lead into the Am chord at bar 4, but as the melody note is also the dominant seventh, the added chord would be redundant.

All these viewpoints are down to musical personal taste.

Understanding the circle of fifths in this way will also help with modulations or key changes during a piece. Modulations are a very useful way of giving your arrangement an extra lift and movement, and are often used for a last verse and chorus, even if it is only a semitone shift; for example, from C major to C# major.

## Creating counter-melodies

Now the chord sequence is more complete, you might find that the melody created by the top notes of the chords is more interesting because of the chord inversions that are used.

Look for patterns of ascending and descending notes within the chords because these can make good counter-melody lines.

A good example is in the first six 'Playground' chords:

| **G** | **D7** | **G** | **C** | **D7** | **G** |
|-------|--------|-------|-------|--------|-------|
| G-B-D | D-F#-A-C | G-B-D | C-E-G | D-F#-A-C | G-B-D |
| **B** | **C** | **D** | **E** | **F#** | **G** |

...which will give you these chord inversions to play:

**Example 11**

22

The top notes of each chord in this progression could be used as a duet part or a counter-melody for live performance, or as part of a sequence.

Here is this counter-melody, notated as a melodic line in the treble clef:

**Example 12**

Compare it with Example 7, which is the equivalent line before the 7<sup>th</sup> chords were added.

## 'On-bass'

There is one more thing to look at when choosing chord inversions with auto accompaniment, and that is the bass line. For organists, this does not present any problems, because the bass pedals are independent from the manuals. For the keyboard player, however, playing a chord that requires a bass note that is not the tonic (or root note) – for example C/G – has, until recently, been impossible.

This became possible with the introduction of a feature called 'on-bass'. Normally, your keyboard scans the left hand notes that you play, and uses the information to confirm which chord is being played. It then automatically adds the correct bass note, which is generally the tonic/root. The 'on-bass' facility is able to identify the lowest note that is being played, and interpret it as the bass note required, thus enabling you to hear the specified bass line.

This makes playing 'on-bass', or slash chords, to give them their commonly-used title, possible. Slash chords show you which bass note the composer/arranger requires; therefore D7/A means play a D7 chord on an A bass note. You would play A as your lowest note of the chord, followed by C, D and F#. C7/G means play a C7 chord on a G bass note, which would be G, Bb, C and E.

A chord symbol on its own means that the bass note is the tonic note of the chord, i.e. 'C' = a C chord on a C bass note.

**Example 13** *(Keyboard)*          **Example 14** *(Organ)*

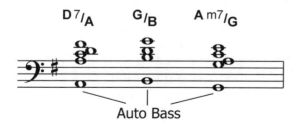

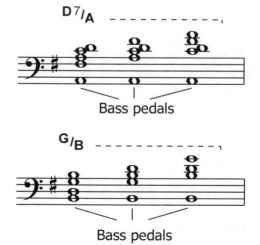

Some manufacturers have even more ways of letting you control the bass notes when you're using the auto accompaniment, so it is worth checking your owner's guide.

As in Example 11, where you were looking for a simple melodic pattern that could form the top notes of your chord sequence, the same idea can work with a bass line too, and can even suggest other chords. For example, here are four bars of 'Playground' with an 'on-bass' chord sequence. Remember that the emphasis now is to produce a melodic bass line rather than a counter-melody.

**Example 15**

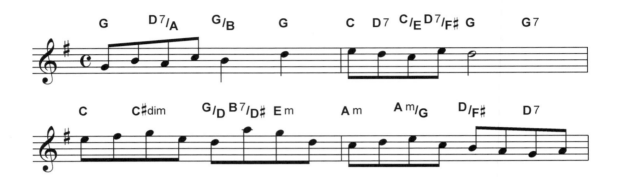

Keyboard players should take note of the following:

- An 'on-bass' note is usually included in the chord that you want to play.

- Because your instrument's 'on-bass' feature recognises the lowest note of your left hand chord as the bass note, you need to ensure that you play the correct chord inversion in order to place the chosen bass note at the bottom of the chord. This requires a change of playing technique, as you can no longer play your basic C major chord in its second inversion. The golden rule of playing all your chords between the two 'F' notes has to be broken. This is another reason why you should be familiar with and understand all your chords in the different positions at all grades.

- In bar 1, a root position G, a second inversion four note D7 and a first inversion G will produce a rising bass line of G, A and B. On beat 4, the root position G chord leads us smoothly to the C chord at the start of bar 2.

- In bar 2, adding an extra D7 and C in their correct inversions will result in a longer rising bass figure from C to G.

- By changing the original D7 in bar three to C#dim (diminished) you can play yet another rising bass line and even though the range is only C to E, it covers every note in between. Diminished chords are very useful for harmonising passing notes or, in this case, for producing a flowing, melodic bass line. To move smoothly from a C to a D in the bass, the only note you can pass through is C#. C# plus the G and E melody notes at beat two in this bar produce a chord of C#dim.

- Bar 4 shows an example of a descending bass line.

Example 16 (on page 25) notates fully these first four bars.

Keyboard players need to play the written inversions, and organ players can use inversions that produce a good counter-melody.

**Example 16**

*NB*: *Rt = root position, 1 = 1st inversion, 2 = 2nd inversion, 3 = 3rd inversion.*

*The notes with the downward stems are bass pedal or auto-bass notes. For keyboard, play the bass clef notes an octave lower than written.*

## Counter-melody

So far, we have concentrated on the relationship between the top note in the chord and the melody note. However, we must also consider the melodic lines that work directly with the written melody for the right hand.

If there is any overriding rule here, it is that whatever notes you decide to play as a harmony note – or notes – should sound musically pleasing to you, and therefore almost anything goes.

Most of us tend to err on the side of caution and stick to something that's more conventional, which is a good idea while you are trying this for the first time. As a guide, if you observe the following points, you should be able to produce some very pleasing results.

- Use your aural skills (listen). What it sounds like is very important.

- Not every melody note needs a separate harmony note.

- The harmony note does not need to be the same rhythm as the melody.

- Except for 'passing notes', take your harmony note from one of the notes of the chord. The more elaborate the chord, the more note choices you'll have.

- Thirds and sixths are the most common harmonising notes and sound rich and warm. Fourths sound quite distant while fifths can sometimes make it difficult to distinguish between the melody and the harmony notes, especially if the sounds being used are similar.

Here is 'Playground' using mainly thirds to harmonise the melody line:

**Example 17**

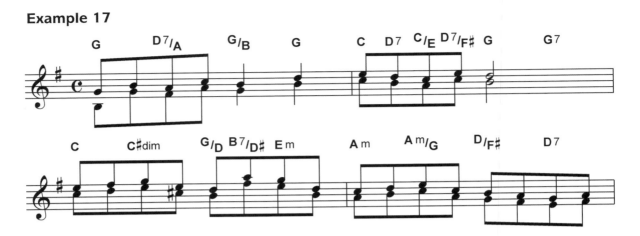

Here is 'Playground' using mainly sixths to harmonise the melody line:

**Example 18**

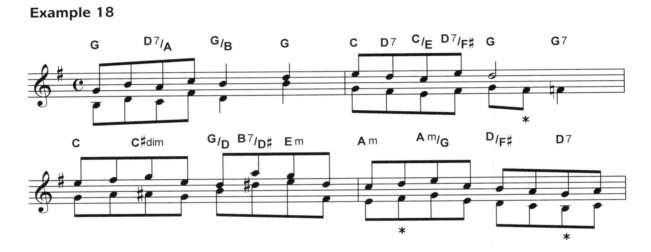

The notes marked * are called passing notes. Passing notes are non-chord notes which pass smoothly between chord notes adding rhythm and interest to the counter-melody.

The following example has a mixture of thirds, sixths and passing notes. Note the additional chords in bar 4, which provide a more melodically interesting bass line.

**Example 19**

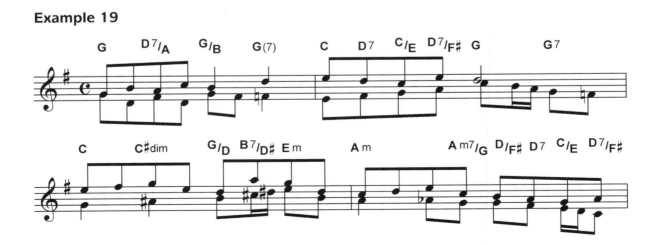

26

You should endeavour to make your harmony notes into a melody of their own, in other words a counter-melody. You will see in this example that the timing does not follow exactly the rhythm of the main tune, and that some extra chords have been added so that the main melody and the counter-melody can flow more easily.

Remember: whatever you choose it is all about personal musical taste – if it works for you, then that is likely to be good enough!

## Chord substitutions

To add extra harmonic colour and musical interest to the chord sequence in your arrangement, it will help to know some basic chord substitutions. Chords can be changed, replaced with others, and even extended to include other notes. It is important to understand that in popular music, a standard chord progression is like a return journey; you leave home, go to your destination via other places before returning home again.

The routes you can take are many and varied, but there are maps to guide you and the intention here is just to give you a few ideas that will encourage and inspire you to explore the possibilities.

There are three main types of chord substitutions:-

- Extensions
- Circular
- Diatonic

## Extensions

A basic major, minor or seventh chord can be enhanced by adding an extra note or notes to extend the harmonic content of the chord; this should not detract from the chord's original function in the chord sequence. The following charts outline the most common extensions:

| CHORD NAME | EXTENSION | SPELLING | STYLE |
|---|---|---|---|
| MAJOR (C) | SIXTH (C6) | 1-3-5-6 | Swing/Jazz & Dance Band |
| | MAJOR SEVENTH (Cmaj7) | 1-3-5-7 | Jazz/Latin & Contemporary Pop Ballads |
| | SEVENTH (C7) | 1-3-5-b7 | Middle of the Road/Latin/Pop Ballads |
| | ADD SECOND (C2) SUSPENDED SECOND (Csus2) | 1-2-5 | Pop Ballads Country/Pop & Church Music |
| | SUSPENDED FOURTH (Csus4) | 1-4-5 | Country/Pop & Church Music |
| | SEVEN SUSPENDED FOURTH (C7sus4) | 1-4-5-b7 | Middle of the Road/Latin/Pop Ballads |
| | AUGMENTED SEVENTH (Caug7) (C+7) | 1-3-#5-b7 | Middle of the Road/Latin/Pop Ballads |
| | SEVEN FLAT FIFTH (C7b5) (C7-5) | 1-3-b5-b7 | Middle of the Road/Latin/Pop Ballads |

| CHORD NAME | EXTENSION | SPELLING | STYLE |
|---|---|---|---|
| | SEVEN SHARP FIFTH (C7#5) (C7+5) | 1-3-#5-b7 | Middle of the Road/Latin/Pop Ballads |
| | SIX/NINE (C6/9) | 1-3-6-9 | Swing/Jazz & Dance Band |
| | MAJOR NINTH (Cmaj9) | 1-3-5-7-9 | Middle of the Road/Latin/Pop Ballads |
| | * NINTH (C9) | 1-3-5-b7-9 | Jazz/Latin & Contemporary Pop Ballads |
| | * ELEVENTH (C11) | 1-b7-9-11 | Jazz/Latin & Contemporary Pop Ballads |
| | * THIRTEENTH (C13) | 1-b7-10-13 | Jazz/Latin & Contemporary Pop Ballads |

| CHORD NAME | EXTENSION | SPELLING | STYLE |
|---|---|---|---|
| MINOR (Cm) | MINOR SIXTH (Cm6) | 1-b3-5-6 | Swing/Jazz & Dance Band |
| | MINOR SEVENTH (Cm7) | 1-b3-5-b7 | Middle of the Road/Latin/Pop Ballads |
| | MINOR-MAJOR SEVENTH (CmM7) | 1-b3-5-7 | Jazz/Latin & Contemporary Pop Ballads |
| | MINOR ADD SECOND (Cm+2) SUSPENDED SECOND (Cmsus2) | 1-2-b3-5 1-2-5 | Pop Ballads Country/Pop & Church Music |
| | SUSPENDED FOURTH (Csus4) | 1-4-5 | Country/Pop & Church Music |
| | MINOR SIX/NINE (Cm6/9) | 1-b3-6-9 | Swing/Jazz & Dance Band |
| | * MINOR NINTH (Cm9) | 1-b3-5-b7-9 | Middle of the Road/Latin/Pop Ballads |
| | MINOR-MAJOR NINTH (CmM9) | 1-b3-5-7-9 | Middle of the Road/Latin/Pop Ballads |

* These chords may only translate correctly when you are using your keyboard in Full Keyboard Mode or on the Organ.

As a general rule, do not substitute:

- major for minor;
- minor for major;
- sixth for seventh (and keep sixths for your swing and dance band songs!)

## Circular

Referring back to the circle of fifths diagram on page 21: if your destination chord is Eb, it is likely to be preceded by Bb7. To make the journey even more interesting, this Bb7 can itself be preceded by the seventh – major or minor – before it. So, your route to Eb can be Fm7 (or F7) > Bb7 > Eb. To get to A, go via Bm7 (or B7) > E7 > A. This is the II-V-I progression commonly found in jazz.

By combining chord extensions and circular substitutions, an interesting route to Bb could be:

| | |
|---|---|
| Normal: | F7 > Bb |
| Add circular: | Cm7 > F7 > Bb |
| Add chord extensions: | Cm9 > F7+5 > Bb6/9 |

This is an exercise that can easily be accomplished on paper and then transferred to the keyboard, and in this way, you can discover new chord progressions without worrying whether or not you actually know the chords – you can always learn them later.

As a further example, let's go back to 'Playground' again and check out some extensions and circular substitutions. Try this also with pieces that you are learning.

### Example 20

## Diatonic

A major scale (which consists of tone, tone, semitone, tone, tone, tone, semitone), such as C major, is called a 'diatonic' scale, and for each note of the scale, you can make four-note chords, built using each third note in the scale. The result will give you the basic chord families for the key of your scale. Here they are for the keys of C and G major.

### Example 21

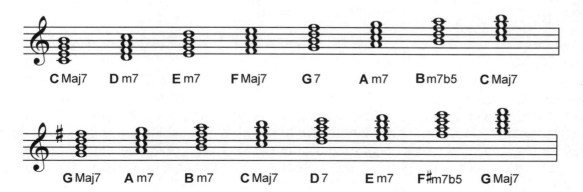

29

These chords are very useful and will create a lot of harmonic interest where the same basic chord is used over several melody notes.

Bar 1 of 'Playground' is a good example of this. As the G chord plays for a whole four beat bar, a diatonic substitution would work like this:

**Example 22**

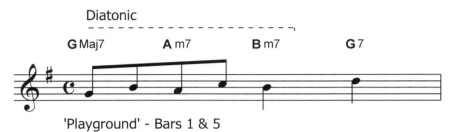

'Playground' - Bars 1 & 5

If you are trying to emulate an easy swing / Latin / 'middle of the road' style of music, you might like to consider using the following ideas to help create some interesting chord substitutions:

- A characteristic of swing style is the use of 6th and 9th chords, and any arrangement that you create featuring this type of chord will automatically give it a dance band feel. Refer to the 'major chords' chart above and you will see in the 'style' column that the 6th and 6/9 chords are suggested for this. 7ths too will benefit from an added 9th.

- The diminished 7th chord (e.g. Cdim7) is an ideal chord for harmonising 'passing' or non-chord notes (notes in the melody that are not part of the supporting chord).

- A diminished 7th chord is made by combining a series of minor third intervals – that is three semitones between each note – until you have a four note chord.

In this example, where one note shares two names, such as F#/Gb or Bb/A# – known as 'enharmonic equivalents' – use the more easily recognised name.

**Example 23**

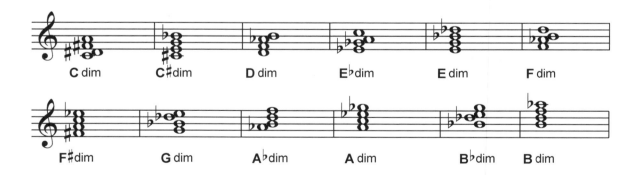

If you investigate these chords, you will discover that the notes which make C diminished are also contained in the Eb, Gb and A diminished chords. C# diminished shares the same notes as E, G and Bb diminished. You will also find the notes for the F, Ab and B diminished chords within the D diminished chord, which therefore suggests that there are actually only three different diminished chord shapes, and it is the inversion that will determine the tonic and, by default, the note name of the chord.

If you add yet another minor third interval to your existing four notes you will arrive at a complete octave. This means that a 'C' diminished chord starting from the bottom up or the top down has the same notes, and it is this element that is useful in finding a chord for a passing note. If your melody note is Bb, then the root of the diminished chord for your passing note is Bb. This can be constructed from the top down – Bb, G, E and C#.

Here is a C major scale – dance band/swing style, using a combination of 6th chords for the basic chord notes and diminished chords for the passing/non-chord notes.

**Example 24**

Here is the result if you apply these dance band extensions and diminished chords to the first two bars of 'Playground'. You will hear that it completely changes the character of the song.

**Example 25**

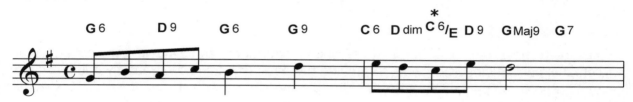

*NB: This chord will probably be displayed on a keyboard's chord display as Am7/E. If you include this 'on-bass' chord, then you must play all the other chords in root position to ensure you hear the correct bass note, unless your instrument has another method of defining it.*

With some of these examples, using auto accompaniment, the chords will not be accessible with your instrument's normal 'fingered' playing mode, because many chords share the same notes played on a different root, as observed with the diminished chords above (see Example 23).

C6 and Am7 share the same note names and it is the root note that will determine the actual chord itself. This makes it impossible for 'fingered' mode to calculate exactly what chord you want it to play. So, to make sure that your instrument recognises as many chords as it can, you need to check in your owner's guide for any specific inversions of these ambiguous chords that the instrument needs you to play in order that you hear your chosen one.

For example, most instruments require that you play all diminished and major or minor 6th chords in root position. You will find, however, that if you use your instrument's 'full keyboard mode', many more chords are recognised.

## Full Keyboard – Fingered Mode

When you select 'Full keyboard mode' the whole of your keyboard (or the entire lower manual of your organ) becomes a chord recognition system. Because you play more notes over a greater area, your instrument has a better chance of calculating the chord. This is also known as 'Pianist mode', the benefits of which will be better realised when you employ a more pianistic approach to harmony (where both hands contribute to a chord).

Examples 13 and 14 on page 23 illustrate a keyboard player and organist's styling, whereas a pianist would play more like this:

**Example 26**

A keyboard player can still utilise these chord extensions, by using a combination of an auto accompaniment in 'fingered mode' to provide the basic rhythm section and by adding some of the extended notes as part of the melody – i.e. playing chords with the right hand. This will simplify the chord sequence, while improving your right hand playing technique. Notated, it will look like this:

**Example 27**

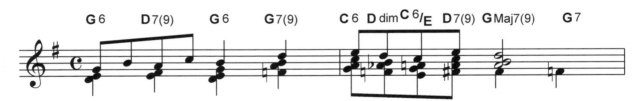

## Conclusion

Finding and creating interesting chord sequences to go with your songs can be an arduous and demanding task; however, the musical satisfaction is a great reward. The choice of chord substitution is, and always will be, a matter of musical taste and, provided that the basis of your substitutions is musically sound, your arrangements will always have the musical edge over a basic lead-sheet arrangement.

There is so much more that can be written about this fascinating subject, which is the very heart of your organ or keyboard – an imitative and expressive music tool. From its keys, sounds, controllers and speakers can come the musical expression of any performer, from the most humble beginner to the accomplished professional.

It is irrelevant that your sounds are imitations of classical instruments, theatre pipe organ, a rock guitar, piano, with auto accompaniments in a diverse selection of styles – it is all music! All these styles have their roots in the basic building blocks of harmony, which is the essence and substance of arranging.

# 3. SEQUENCING

This chapter explains the role of the 'sequencer', 'song creator' or 'song recorder' and how it can be used musically to enhance a performance. When recording a performance into a 'sequencer', 'song creator' or 'song recorder' the term 'programming' is the industry standard and although this can conjure up thoughts of robotic music, it is fair to state that a sequence is only as musical as the musician who programmed it.

It is often suggested that using a sequence as part of a live performance is cheating. In reality, however, performing with a musically creative sequence requires an advanced level of musicianship. 'Techno fear' has also generated the accusation of cheating, but whether or not you agree with these sentiments, this type of music technology is here to stay, and as a serious music student, it is important that you should be familiar with the fundamentals of sequencing and acquire the skills necessary to be confident in using this technology musically and creatively, in order to enhance your live performances (as opposed to making a performance easier).

Controversy regarding new technology is not exclusive to the 21st century, and we should be thankful that the great composers of the past pushed the creative boundaries by using modern technology, rather than being afraid of it, otherwise we would probably still be playing dulcimers, harpsichords, viols and sackbuts.

J. S. Bach (1685-1750) and Ludwig van Beethoven (1770-1827) were just two composers who used the latest technology. In Bach's day, the organ and pianoforte (for which Bach wrote his 'Well Tempered Klavier' of 1722/1744) were just as new as the modern keyboards of today. Beethoven introduced a new instrument to the symphony orchestra during the last movement of his 5th Symphony (1808) – the trombone.

If these great composers were around today, they would without doubt be using new technology and pushing the boundaries of musical creativity.

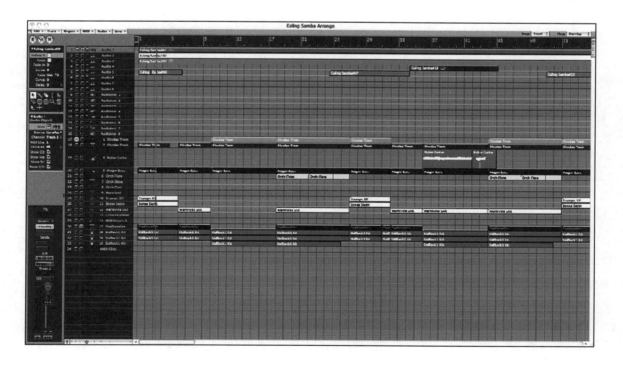

*A typical Logic Pro sequence*

## The sequencer

There are two types of sequencer with which you can create a sequence:

- The on-board sequencer built into your instrument;
- External software such as Logic 7, Cubase or Sonar which you would use with a Mac or PC.

Each of the above will give you 16 independent tracks, which can be controlled for sound, volume and DSP effects (see p39). This means you could have 16 different sounds being played alongside the other sounds you choose to play live with two hands, and in the case of the organ, pedals. The only restriction is the polyphony of your particular instrument. Polyphony is the total amount of notes that your instrument is capable of generating simultaneously. This can be anything from 32 up to 128 notes depending on the age and make of the instrument.

External software, linked by MIDI (Musical Instrument Digital Interface) to your instrument, is probably the most versatile way of creating a sequence, as the editing facilities, together with the ability to print out your sequence in music notation afterwards, are far more flexible. This software is readily available, and although the full professional packages may be out of your budget, both Logic and Cubase offer lighter packages, namely Logic Express and Cubase Lite.

Sequencer and digital audio packages offer an unlimited amount of tracks for programming. However, when creating a MIDI file for use with your instrument, you are limited to the amount of tracks your instrument can play – normally 16 tracks. Using this type of software is ideal for those whose instrument does not have an on-board sequencer, but has the facility to play MIDI files.

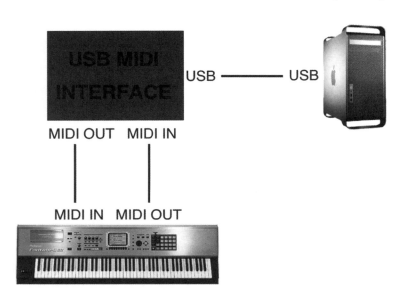

Connecting a computer to your instrument is straightforward – you will need either two MIDI leads or, if your instrument and PC are USB-compatible, a USB lead. Most modern computers have USB ports, so if your instrument does not have USB, you will also need a USB-MIDI interface, available from most good music shops.

Once connected, the software's installation guide will then outline how to match the MIDI channels to the individual tracks and show you what to do in order to start programming.

The on-board sequencer is often much easier to use, but from an editing point of view can be quite limited. Whichever method you choose, the aim is to create a realistic musical sequence that will enhance a live performance.

## Getting started

How do you start to program a creative sequence that will enhance a live performance?

First of all you need an arrangement (see Chapter 2: Arranging), a musical plan outlining how many bars the performance will be, and an understanding of the style of music you are trying to produce, be it a full classical symphony, dixieland jazz or modern pop. A good analogy to explain this is that of building a house. Builders don't just start laying bricks, they work with a plan, a design drawn up by an architect. In musical terms, the architect is the arranger, the builder is the programmer and the architect's design is the arrangement.

In this chapter, 'track' is used to refer to the physical 16 tracks on your instrument's sequencer, and 'part' refers to the individual instrument sounds being used in your arrangement. Once you have arranged your piece of music, your architect's plan in hand, you can commence programming.

## Programming methods

There are two methods of programming a sequence – Step Time and Real Time.

**Step Time** programming can be very time consuming, as each individual note is entered separately, along with the note's length and its velocity (volume). The end result is very unnatural and unmusical, and as a consequence, will sound very computerised. This type of programming is fine for those who, for whatever reason, can only make music in this way, but for the serious music student, it should be avoided.

There are two exceptions to this: recording either a rhythm track using the preset auto accompaniments (programmed rhythm patterns), or a left hand chord sequence. This is perfectly acceptable, because all you are doing is instructing the sequencer to play a particular rhythm pattern or chord sequence for so many bars. As the rhythm pattern or auto accompaniment is already musical, programming in this way does not decrease the musicality – it is also the quickest method for programming a rhythm sequence. The use of 'step record' in this way is only possible using the on-board sequencer in your instrument, as auto accompaniment patterns are not always transmitted by MIDI, and would therefore not always work with a software sequencer. It is the recommended way for programming the rhythm track for Grades 1 to 3.

**Real Time** programming is exactly that – in real time. For example, if you stop playing for two minutes when programming, on replay, the sequence would have a gap of two minutes, exactly at the place at which you stopped playing.

The main advantage of real time is that the sequencer records not only the notes you play, but also the way you played them, capturing every nuance. This method of programming requires 100% accuracy of performance, as the sequencer will not correct any wrong notes or rhythmic mistakes. It can usually be edited later, allowing the correction of notes or tidying up of rhythm passages with quantizing.

Real time programming with just a small amount of editing, or preferably none, will guarantee you a musical and natural performance.

## Editing

Software packages offer in-depth editing facilities, and most on-board sequencers will offer the basic editing tools such as altering notes, their length and velocity (volume). This type of editing can be very useful when you have finished recording what appeared to be a near perfect take, only to find on playback that there were one or two wrong notes, or that a few notes were slightly louder or shorter than the rest. Be careful, however, as over-editing can turn a very live musical sequence into one with a computerised, robotic sound.

To find out what editing facilities your instrument has and how to operate them, you should consult your teacher or the owner's manual.

## Quantizing

Quantizing is a way of correcting rhythmic inaccuracies by setting a minimum note duration. It is particularly useful when programming drum parts, as this will help keep the part rhythmically tight. Most in-built sequencers will allow quantizing. You need to set the quantize value to the shortest note length within the part you wish to quantize. For example, if the shortest note length in the part is a quaver, then setting the quantize value to a quaver will automatically change any notes which are shorter (e.g. a semiquaver) into a quaver. You can set the quantize value before or after you have recorded your part, but be careful when quantizing anything other than a drum part. As with over-editing, this can make a live musical performance sound robotic.

## So how do you start?

Having prepared the arrangement, including the amount of parts you are going to use and the method of programming, the first track to be programmed should be the drums/rhythm part. This is musically logical, as these parts are normally present throughout an arrangement and will therefore give your sequence a start and finish point – an outline on which you build the rest of your sequence, like the foundations of a house (you don't build a house starting with the roof!).

The type of drum/rhythm part to be programmed depends on the grade. For Grades 1 to 3, a preset auto accompaniment is the easiest way of starting a sequence, as this will automatically include a bass part. All you may need to add is a counter-melody that simply takes a note from the chords you are playing. (See Chapter 2: Arranging). From Grade 4 upwards, you will most likely want to program the drums separately, as opposed to using a preset auto accompaniment pattern.

Having completed the rhythm track, you now have something to play along with and keep in time with, rather like a metronome. The next track to program is the bass part. Choose the desired track and the bass sound you wish to use. If no rhythm part is required, the bass part will be the first.

If you are using the on-board sequencer in your instrument, then press 'Record' and 'Synchro start', as this will start the sequencer when you play the first bass note. If the bass part does not start from bar 1, then simply start the sequencer by pressing 'Start'. Whichever method you use, you will hear the rhythm track playing back, so be ready to come in at the right place with your bass part. Remember that either type of sequencer will record every nuance, so your bass part performance needs to be live.

If you are using software, then simply press 'Record' and the sequence will start to play. You also have the luxury with software and with top of the range instruments to give yourself one or two bars count-in.

Which track you use for which part is entirely your own choice; there are no hard and fast rules, although all commercially available SMF MIDI files use a standardised track allocation with drums on track 10 and the melody assigned to track 4. For a more detailed specification on SMF MIDI files visit: www.midi.org/about-midi/gm/gm1sound.shtml

Having completed the drums/rhythm and bass tracks you can then add whichever extra tracks you feel your arrangement needs, be it counter-melodies or extra harmonies, using exactly the same routine. Always keep in mind your live parts at this point, as you need to ensure that any counter-melodies or harmonies actually support the melody, and that they do not interfere with or overcrowd your live parts. You can record a melody guide track, which can be deleted later, to assist with this.

Choose the next track, sound, etc., and each time you program a new track, you will hear the tracks you have already programmed. Your sequencer will also remember the sound you used. This is because each sound on your digital instrument is given a 'program change' number which is stored at the start of the track, and during the track if you change sound while programming. Other performance data such as volume, reverb, and DSP effects is also stored in the same way. This data is saved on completion of the track, so that each time you play it back, you will hear the same sounds and effects. This is very useful as it saves setting it up every time, and while programming, it allows you to judge exactly how your sequence is progressing. Depending on your instrument's specification, you may be able to fine-tune this performance data once you have completed your sequence.

A good piece of advice is to remember that 'less is more'. It is very easy to get carried away, using all 16 tracks, but quite often just an added counter-melody with a few supporting harmonies can be effective and very musical.

Completing your sequenced masterpiece is only the beginning of your enhanced live performance. The next part requires musicianship of the highest standard, as your live performance must be 100% accurate, every time. If you skip a beat or stop, your sequenced masterpiece won't wait for you. This is a great discipline to master, as it is just like playing with 'real life' musicians.

## Colla voce style

The sequences discussed so far have involved a constant pulse or tempo from a drum/rhythm track, but what about programming a sequence that requires no drums/rhythm, in a 'colla voce tempo' style?

*Colla voce* (It.) literally means 'with voice', indicating to an accompanist, for example, to take the tempo from the soloist. In other words, it is a phrase or passage with a free tempo and would therefore not work with an auto-accompaniment style.

This is more complex, and requires a little more thought and advanced musicianship. In this scenario, once you have completed your arrangement, you should start by programming the solo melody part – in other words the part you will perform live, with all the nuances of a live performance. This then gives you your outline, with the start and finish of the live performance and all your natural tempo changes. However, when programming this style of sequence it is important to remember that your sequence cannot be quantized at any point, as the sequencer is running in free time. You must also remember to turn off the metronome feature when recording, as you will find it impossible to play freely against the solid pulse of a metronome beat.

Having completed your live performance, while the sequencer replays it, you can program your accompanying parts. When you are happy with the finished sequence, simply delete your live performance data, which will leave you with just the sequenced accompanying parts.

The level of musicianship required to perform with a sequence of this nature is quite advanced and this type of performance would only be expected from Grade 6 upwards. But don't let that put you off – the sooner you start, the more experienced and confident you'll become.

## Control track

Another feature of the sequencer which candidates of all grades should be capable of programming and using, is a 'control' track. A control track stores control data, and will replay the data as and when you require it throughout your live performance.

A control track is a digital recording of buttons being pressed at specific points during your piece – it is like having someone sitting next to you pressing all the buttons which, in an ideal world you would be if only you had four hands during your performance. This might include things like a registration change at bar 16, or the fill in the bar before registration change no. 4 which you always forget, because there just is not time. The control track can do all of this for you.

It is quite simple to program, as, in programming terms, it requires no notes to be played. In 'real time' record mode, simply press the control buttons you would press during a live performance, such as auto accompaniment changes, registration changes, tempo and volume changes, transposition, etc. – in fact, any control data that you require during your performance.

This is normally programmed in real time, but can easily be done in step time, and can be as simple or as complex as you wish. Whether or not you are only programming a control track, you will still need an outline to work with, preferably with the changes carefully marked so you know exactly what you require and when. You can then either program the live melody line, and make your control changes while this is being replayed, or alternatively, you can simply start the chosen auto accompaniment (with the intro if you are using one) and then while you follow the arrangement through, make your control changes. Remember to choose an ending or stop the auto accompaniment once your arrangement has finished. This process can also be used to record your chosen auto accompaniment and any intro/ending being used, along with the control data.

When completed, the control track can be replayed independently without the need for any other track. As with all sequences, there is of course one drawback, which is that once the sequence is playing, your live performance has to be 100% accurate, otherwise you will have control data changes occurring at the wrong time and in the wrong places.

## Mixing

When you have finished programming your arrangement, there is one more process that needs to be completed, in order to turn an average arrangement into a musical masterpiece – and that is mixing.

It is advisable to do the mix a couple of days after finishing the programming, because you will approach the mixing with a fresh pair of ears, as they can get very tired after a long programming session. All commercial CDs are recorded and then mixed and mastered at a later date, so why should your arrangement be any different?

It must be said that the art of mixing cannot be learnt from reading a book; it comes with experience, an in-depth knowledge of your instrument, and by listening carefully using your aural skills. However, the fundamentals are easy to understand.

*A typical Logic Pro mixer*

## Achieving a good balance

Once you have completed all of your tracks, the first thing to check is that the volume levels of each track have a nice balance with your live performance. Most modern instruments will allow you to alter the volume of each track independently and so, using your aural skills, a good balance should be easy to achieve.

*NB: Resist the temptation to keep turning volumes up on parts – turn the others down.*

## Adding DSP effects

DSP (Digital Signal Processing) effects are those subtle effects that can make all the difference when mixing your arrangement. For example, an electric piano without chorus can sound a little bland and uninteresting, but with chorus, the sound becomes alive, musical and animated with a lovely rich and warm timbre. Another example would be to add distortion to an electric guitar if you are aiming for a heavy metal feel, but whatever the effect, don't use too much as this can have an adverse effect. There are no rules or set parameters regarding the use of DSP effects, and although the manufacturers' default settings are normally quite acceptable, don't let this stop you from experimenting with original sounds, as this is how you gain valuable experience.

Reverb is another DSP effect which can make an enormous amount of difference to your finished sequence. Reverb is an electronically simulated sound of an acoustic space. For instance, when you walk into a room that is covered in carpet, with curtains, furniture, etc., and talk or sing, the acoustic is very dry – there are no echoes or reverberation, as the fabrics in the room soak up the sound reflections. However, in a large church or concert hall where the space is much bigger, with very little (if any) fabric, the sound echoes and reverberates much more, making the sound appear 'bigger' than it actually is.

This simulated effect, be it 'room', 'stage', 'concert hall' or 'cathedral', adds another dimension when creating a realistic musical performance. Obviously, you would be unlikely to have a trad. jazz band or hip-hop arrangement using a cathedral setting, but again there are no hard or fast rules regarding the use of reverb: just use your aural skills to decide which setting best suits your particular arrangement.

## The Stereo Image

When you listen to any recorded stereo source – be it CD, record or MP3 player – the stereo image is the simulation of where the sounds appear in the live performance. For example, in a live string orchestra (looking from the audience) the violin section is generally positioned to the left of the conductor, with the violas in the centre and the cellos and basses on the right. Therefore when this is recorded, you will hear the violins appear to come from the left speaker with the violas centrally and cellos and basses more from the right speaker. This separation or placement of each sound is commonly known as the 'stereo image'. To ensure that your sequence is as live and realistic as possible, this can be replicated when programming.

# DRUM KIT STEREO IMAGE

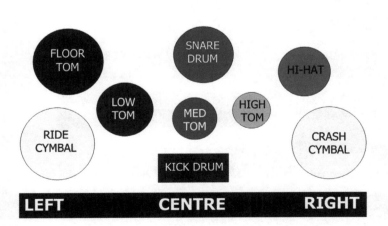

Placing your sounds within the stereo image will also create a bigger sound spectrum from your instrument, giving it a professional CD-quality production. This facility is known as 'panning', and the pan control is normally found on the mixer page within either the software you are using, or on your keyboard or organ. It is also important to pan the drum kit, where possible, to the standard format. The diagrams on the next page illustrate just three examples of where instruments would sit on a live stage and where they usually appear within the stereo image.

# SYMPHONY ORCHESTRA

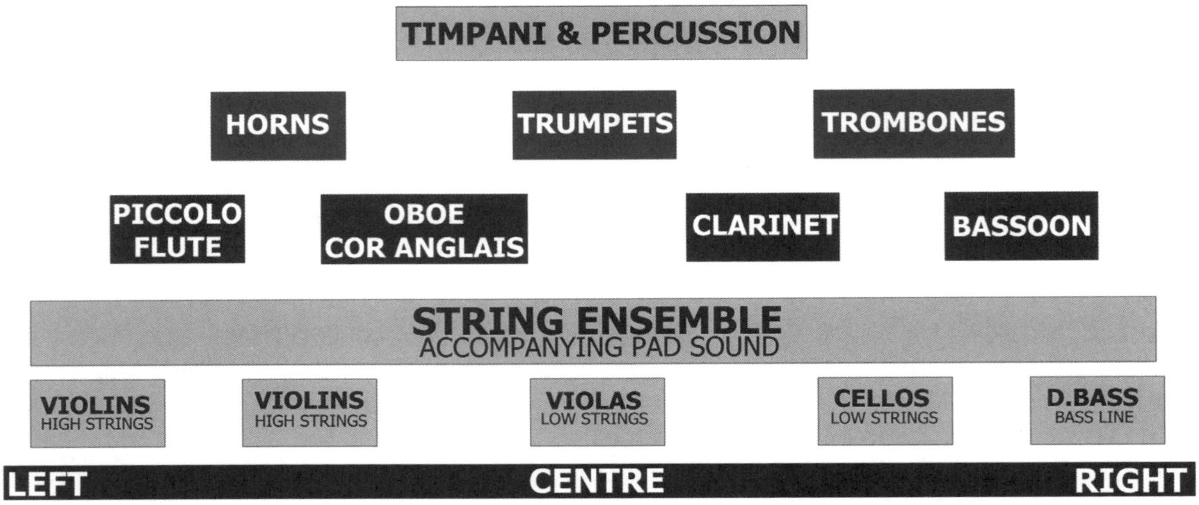

TIMPANI & PERCUSSION

HORNS | TRUMPETS | TROMBONES

PICCOLO FLUTE | OBOE COR ANGLAIS | CLARINET | BASSOON

**STRING ENSEMBLE**
ACCOMPANYING PAD SOUND

| VIOLINS HIGH STRINGS | VIOLINS HIGH STRINGS | VIOLAS LOW STRINGS | CELLOS LOW STRINGS | D.BASS BASS LINE |

LEFT — CENTRE — RIGHT

# BIG BAND

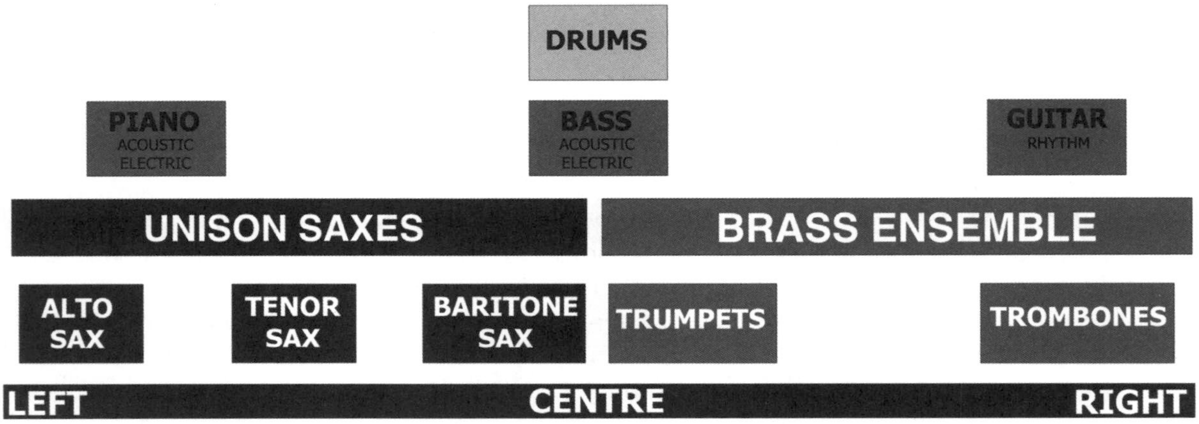

DRUMS

PIANO ACOUSTIC ELECTRIC | BASS ACOUSTIC ELECTRIC | GUITAR RHYTHM

UNISON SAXES | BRASS ENSEMBLE

| ALTO SAX | TENOR SAX | BARITONE SAX | TRUMPETS | TROMBONES |

LEFT — CENTRE — RIGHT

# FILM/TV THEME ORCHESTRA

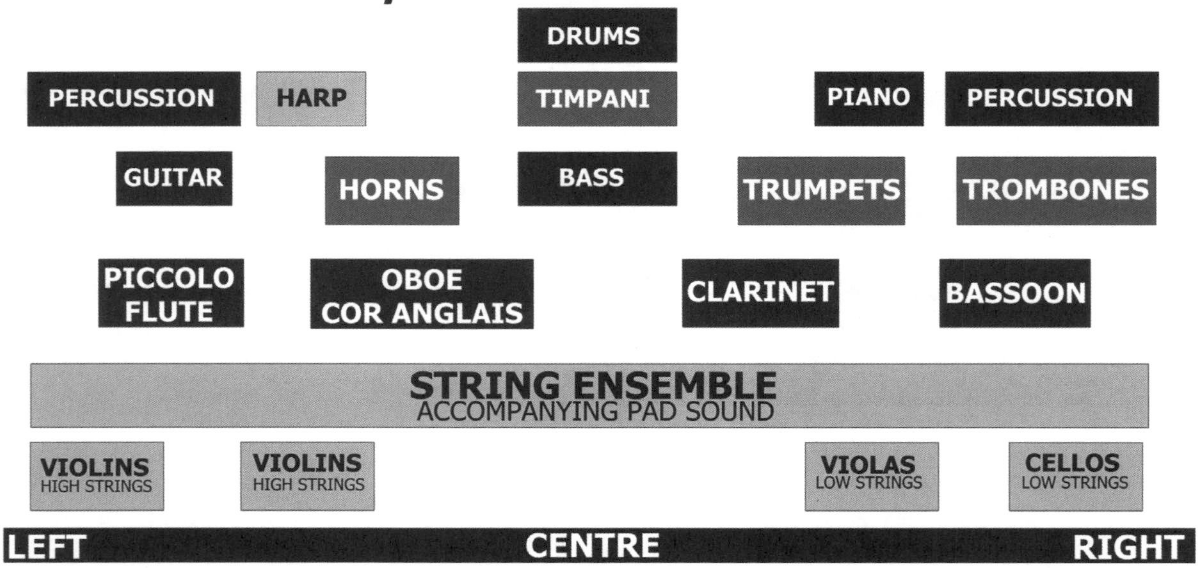

DRUMS

PERCUSSION | HARP | TIMPANI | PIANO | PERCUSSION

GUITAR | HORNS | BASS | TRUMPETS | TROMBONES

PICCOLO FLUTE | OBOE COR ANGLAIS | CLARINET | BASSOON

**STRING ENSEMBLE**
ACCOMPANYING PAD SOUND

| VIOLINS HIGH STRINGS | VIOLINS HIGH STRINGS | VIOLAS LOW STRINGS | CELLOS LOW STRINGS |

LEFT — CENTRE — RIGHT

# 4. PROGRAMMING ACCOMPANIMENT STYLES

This chapter explores the orchestrated accompaniments that work in conjunction with, and are triggered by, your left hand chords – they are your 'backing' band or orchestra, over which you play your piece. A thorough understanding of how and why these auto accompaniments work will certainly add to your own creativity, and greatly influence the way you actually perform your pieces. It will also encourage you to program your own very specific individual accompaniment styles, especially for the higher grades, and providing your instrument has the facility.

## Auto accompaniments

'Auto accompaniment' – generally referred to as 'styles', 'patterns' or 'backings' – has been the subject of some of the most significant musical advances in organ and keyboard design. The quality of writing for these orchestrated accompaniments is complemented by the greatly improved sound samples available to composers of these styles. The improved sound also makes the styles more realistic than ever before, and because of this they have encouraged a new generation of musicians to create 'real' arrangements for these instruments. The accompaniment styles, particularly the intros and endings, are commissioned musical compositions, written by professional musicians and are not the work of computer generation. Moreover, these styles accurately reflect what happens in an actual band or group; therefore, much can be learnt about the work of musicians and how they work together as a team, simply by studying your instrument's accompaniments.

If you listen to one of your instrument's accompaniment styles, particularly one of the more elaborate ones, you will hear that there are four elements involved: drums and percussion, bass, instruments playing rhythmically, and instruments playing sustained chords or counter-melodies. The actual notes that you will hear depends upon the left hand chord that is being played, together with the way that your particular brand of instrument recognises the notes in that chord. Some instruments simply strum or sustain the notes that you are physically playing, whereas some systems will scan the notes that you play, decipher the chord, and then produce an accompaniment based on what a real backing band would play in that style.

In the case of more musically creative instruments, this can be most effective, especially if you are using standard 'fingered' left hand chords which only recognise the more basic chord types. A C major chord in a swing or jazz style will probably feature 6th notes and 9th notes, whereas the same chord in a country style or contemporary ballad will have additional 2nd notes and suspended 4th notes (see Chapter 2: Arranging). In both cases, extra notes are added by your auto accompaniment system to create realism, because, as already mentioned, these accompaniments are based on musical reality and not a computer engineer's vision of it.

Auto accompaniment or rhythm pattern writing is an art in itself, and a better quality instrument will reward you with superior accompaniments. These are created to accommodate most chord types, and on some instruments will play different patterns in different keys, so that a style variation playing an Eb chord will not be the same if you play an Ab chord. A top of the range instrument will have specific major and minor intros and endings, rather than just flattening the third of the major version. These are only a couple of examples of how manufacturers are improving the musicality of their instruments; there are many more.

Having established that auto accompaniments are actually small musical compositions in their own right, it means that a musician employed by a manufacturer to create these accompaniments will write their own arrangement of that style. Therefore, each manufacturer's 8-beat will be slightly different; the style will be that of an 8-beat, but the phrasing and instrumentation will be subtly altered to create a unique pattern. Thus we cannot study the definitive 8-beat accompaniment style, because there isn't one.

All styles have a general make-up, as well as some specific requirements, and it is the generic pattern of six different accompaniment styles that we will look at. When studying the following examples, it is important to remember that you are looking at what your accompaniment style is likely to play, based on a chord of C major. Add a 7th and you will either hear an added note, or the chord's root or 5th will be transposed to form the 7th. If a minor chord is played, then the 3rd will be flattened, or a slightly different pattern will be heard. Some keyboards have specific patterns for other chords, such as diminished chords, but the examples here are based on the most common patterns.

### Drum notation

In the LCM Grade 5 handbook for keyboard (LL176) there is a percussion study which is written using drum notation, 'In the Groove'. As drums do not have a definite pitch, each line of the stave is allocated to an instrument. For example, the hi-hat is notated above the top line and to indicate that this is the hi-hat, the note head is a cross. The bass drum uses the bottom space and a traditional note head, as do the snare (3rd space up) and tom toms. To help with reading, and being able to construct a drum part, the examples in this chapter use this standard drum notation:

### Six generic accompaniment styles

There are many different accompaniment styles ranging from traditional rhythms through to the more up to date drum & bass, trance, hip-hop, rap and dance patterns. However, as with most musical things, if you have a good knowledge of the basics, then understanding the more complex rhythms becomes much easier. The six generic accompaniment styles being used as examples are also rhythms which are most commonly used in the early grades. The six generic accompaniment styles are:

- 8-beat
- Waltz
- 2/4 march
- Swing
- Shuffle
- Beguine

## 8-beat

This is the most widely used 'straight eight' (as opposed to swing or 'rolling eighths') accompaniment style and is suitable for most 'middle of the road' pop, easy listening and country pieces. It is a simple style, with quavers giving the rhythm its easy movement – hence the name.

Here is the drum pattern for a basic 8-beat variation. Notice the hi-hat accents which fall on beats two and four, highlighting the 'off' beats. These are also the beats on which the snare drum plays.

### Example 28: 8-beat drum part

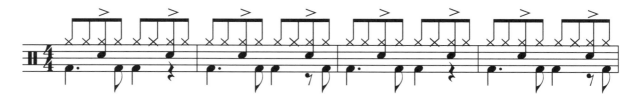

Your auto accompaniment system will add other musical parts. Here is the bass guitar part, which, as part of the rhythm section, plays the same kind of rhythm as the bass drum.

### Example 29: 8-beat bass part

Part of the style will be some kind of rhythm or accented (mute) guitar part. It will be similar to the following example, which as you can see plays mainly on the 'off' beats, just like the snare drum.

### Example 30: 8-beat rhythm guitar part

*NB: The dots above the notes mean that you play the notes in a short detached manner (staccato). The short horizontal line above the notes mean that you should give the note its full value (tenuto).*

There will almost certainly be a strummed guitar part in the style as well, using the sound of either a 12-string or steel strung folk guitar. Again, the accents fall on the 'off' beats and the notated part looks like this:

### Example 31: 8-beat strummed guitar part

In addition to the drums and bass, most instruments will have at least three other parts with which to create a style. The two guitar parts shown here are rhythmic, so it's likely that any further parts will be either sustained chords – usually referred to as pad sounds – or some kind of melodic line (counter-melody). This could be a finger style guitar, a piano or perhaps strings playing single notes.

Here is an example of a piano part:

### Example 32: 8-beat piano part

And so that you can see how everything fits together, here are all the parts in a full score:

**Example 33: 8-beat full score**

## Waltz

The waltz is a style that has three crotchet beats in each bar, rather than the more common four, and there are many different versions of it:

- English
- Viennese
- Jazz
- Chanson

They are all derivatives of the basic 'one, two, three – one, two, three' feel, and probably its most popular version will be found in the ballroom section of your accompaniment styles. You will also find this three beat rhythm in pop, country and movie genres, so do not think of it as just an old-fashioned strict tempo dance.

Although this style has a definite 'lilt', in a traditional waltz, all the main notes fall on either a crotchet or quaver beat, with the accent falling on the first beat of the bar (the 'down' beat), followed by the weaker second and third beats. There can also be a slight emphasis on beat three, which leads the rhythm more easily into the next bar.

Here is a basic drum pattern using just the bass drum, snare drum and open and closed hi-hat.

**Example 34: waltz drum part**

A hi-hat is a pair of cymbals that open and close via a foot pedal. There are two main ways in which they are used:

- Pressing the pedal will bring the cymbals together producing a kind of 'tch' sound which is usually for the 'off' beats. This is called closed hi-hat and is notated +.

- The hi-hat can also be hit with a drumstick. With the cymbals closed you hear a metallic 'tapping' sound and with the hi-hat half open, you will hear a longer 'tshshsh' sound. Open hi-hat is notated o.

Unlike the short rhythmic bass notes in the 8-beat style, the waltz bass line has longer notes with less movement. The main notes start on beat one (the 'down' beat) with pick-up notes at the end of bars 2 and 4.

**Example 35: waltz bass part**

The standard tempo for a waltz is 90 bpm, which is quite slow and stately, thus giving room for lots of expression within the accompaniment pattern. Many instruments will take advantage of this and actually program a slight 'strum' on a rhythm guitar part. This could be done equally as well using a piano or harp sound, with the chords playing on beats two and three like this:

**Example 36: waltz rhythm guitar part**

Generally a waltz is considered to be a romantic style, and therefore an orchestration featuring piano and strings is assumed to be the norm. The piano will usually play a simple broken chord phrase like this:

**Example 37: waltz piano part**

with strings playing sustained chords like this:

**Example 38: waltz string / pad part**

The simple 'pad' strings part is most effective in making the overall pattern sound smooth and flowing, giving a good contrast against the rhythmic parts.

So that you can see how the individual parts integrate, here they are in full score form:

**Example 39: waltz full score**

## 2/4 March

Marches are generally written with a two beat feel, and when considering the music's original purpose (that of soldiers marching in time), it would seem the most natural option. Marches are often written in other time signatures, like 4/4, 6/8 and 'cut common' (alla breve), yet all have that 'one two – one two' motion.

Most marches feature predominantly brass instruments of all kinds, with more recent arrangements adding saxophones as in orchestral wind bands. Flutes, piccolos and the ornate bell lyre are also an integral part of the instrumental line-up, particularly in a marching band because these high pitched sounds carry so well. The example here is an intermediate level, standard American style 2/4 march, the tempo for which is around 112bpm.

The drum sounds for a marching band do not come from a traditional drum kit, but from individually carried drums and cymbals. Depending on the size of the band, there will be a large pair of hand held crash cymbals, a large bass drum, a triangle and two or more snare (or side) drums. Their respective sounds are bigger and brighter than the drum kit counterparts.

Example 40 shows the drum and percussion parts. As you can see, the rhythm is very simple, with everything playing the two main pulses except the snare drum(s) which play on the 'off' beat. This gives the accompaniment style a strong direction and will encourage you to phrase your music in a march-like manner. Notice that the notation is different from a standard drum part – this is because each instrument is played by a separate person, therefore each player needs an individual part.

## Example 40: march drum part

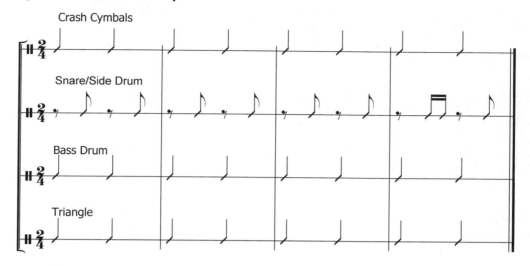

The bass line is also different. In the 8-beat and waltz styles, the bass is mainly playing the chord's root note, but in the march, the bass now plays a traditional 'root – fifth' pattern. Notice the 'pick-up' notes to the next phrase at the end of bar 4.

Another major difference is in the instrumentation. Obviously, when marching, a band cannot use a bass guitar or double bass, so normally a tuba, or in American marching bands, a sousaphone, is employed.

## Example 41: march tuba part

The main instrumental rhythmic parts are split between the trumpets, which play the higher chord notes, and the trombones playing the lower chord notes. Duplication of notes often occurs, and this helps to create a solid 'off' beat which is further accented by the snare drum. To enable you to see the composition of the brass chords, here are the trumpet and trombone parts together:

## Example 42: march brass parts

To add an element of extra movement and brightness to the ensemble, flutes and piccolos often play light counter-melodies, trills and turns. This fits well with the way in which accompaniment styles are programmed, and here is a typical example of what a woodwind combination might play:

## Example 43: march flute part

Finally, to add a touch of gravity to this rhythmic 2/4 march, French horns, playing mainly sustained chords, can be added. If your auto accompaniment system has enough parts, you will probably find this horn line in one of the extra parts.

A typical French horn part would be as follows:

**Example 44: march French horn part**

The 2/4 march is a good style to help build a sense of how the beats in a bar actually work. It drives you along and can really help you establish a good rhythmic foundation.

Here are all the march parts in full score form:

**Example 45: march full score**

## Swing

Think of 'Little Brown Jug', 'In The Mood', 'Mack The Knife' or 'American Patrol': these are classic examples of the swing style. Slow and romantic or fast bebop, the basic rhythm is the same and, simple as it is, not everyone adapts naturally to playing in this style. Whereas the styles that we have studied so far can be understood just by being able to count quavers/eighth notes, the 4/4 swing style relies on displaced second quaver notes in beats two and four to give a sense of, not quite syncopation, but more of a quaver triplet, which might be notated thus:

**Example 46**

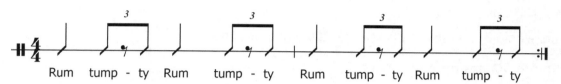

The normal pulses for this style are the 'off' beats on two and four, and Example 47 shows the rhythm that is played by the drummer on open and closed hi-hat or ride cymbal. A drum stick laid horizontally across the snare drum to strike the drum's rim (rim shot) is a common sound for the two and four 'off' beats, while the bass drum will play either on beats one and three or on the first crotchet note in every other bar. The latter will produce a more open and less regimented swing.

Here is how the swing style drum pattern looks:

**Example 47: swing drum part**

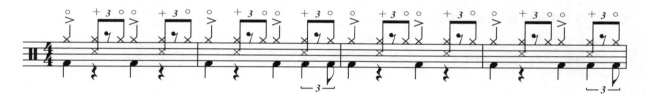

*NB: The rim shot shares the same space on the stave as the snare drum, but the note-head is changed to a cross.*

The bass line for this style works with the drums to drive the rhythm along. This type of swing bass line is commonly known as a 'walking bass' (because of its regular 'walking' structure up and down a chord or scale, regarded as the archetypal swing bass) or as a 'four in a bar' bass.

The example here is just one of many smooth sounding 'four in a bar' bass figures which are either based on a 6th chord, or the scale tones with passing notes using an acoustic bass (see Chapter 7: Instruments and Suggested Listening).

**Example 48: swing bass part**

Also helping to give impetus to the rhythm is the guitar. This is usually played on a steel strung semi-acoustic instrument. The four-in-a-bar 'long, short, long, short' rhythm with accented 'off' beat is a swing band rhythm section's mainstay. In Example 49, notice the tenuto and staccato accent marks which give the player a clear indication of how the phrase is to be articulated:

**Example 49: swing guitar part**

If your instrument's auto accompaniment system has more than three melodic parts, it is likely to add a fourth member to the rhythm section, namely, the pianist. With a guitar strumming a regular 'four in a bar', the piano is now free to add a degree of punctuation to the rhythm, by playing a mixture of held chords and accented 'stabs' – usually when there is a melodic gap or when other sections are not playing.

Here's an example of a four-bar phrase that demonstrates this:

**Example 50: swing piano part**

The brass section, whether trumpets, trombones or a mixture of both, will add dynamic chord 'shouts' to a rhythmic accompaniment. (Don't forget that you are just accompanying here – not playing the tune; your right hand is doing that with its own instrumental sounds).

This example is a standard swing band phrase, and it is likely to be featured in one of your instrument's swing accompaniment styles, maybe with the first chord in bars 2 and 4 playing through the two following rests.

**Example 51: swing brass part**

Even though your accompaniment styles will play mainly rhythmic patterns, certain instruments will play sustained notes, which will help the pattern flow more smoothly. These sustained notes, although not quite a counter-melody, will change as you change the chords and, if the note is the chord's tonic (as in this example), the harmony's tonality is better established, as well as giving the accompaniment a strong foundation. A sound you could use for this part is *Unison Saxes*.

**Example 52: swing sax part**

There are so many variations on the swing theme that the example here can only convey a tiny aspect of it; yet if you spend time listening to the different swing and jazz styles that appear on your instrument, you will almost certainly hear all of the phrases shown here.

Here are all of the swing parts for you to study:

**Example 53: swing full score**

## Shuffle

The shuffle is an extension of the swing style and tends to be more driving and dynamic. Its roots are in the fifties from around the time that big band swing and bebop were fading in popularity, so this was 'swing for a younger audience'. Shuffle uses the same 'rolling eighths' concept as swing, but the accompaniment is generally much busier than a 'laid-back' swing pattern, and has lots of room for individual improvisation from the rhythm section.

Here is just one example of a drums shuffle pattern. You will see the familiar off-beat accents for the hi-hat and snare drum playing opposite an insistent accented bass drum on the one and three downbeats. A hi-hat variation might be to play each quarter note via a quick press and half release of its pedal, which lets the cymbals touch but still ring out; this allows the drummer two hands for the snare drum. Also, the hi-hat rhythm, as written here, could be played on a tambourine, adding even more drive to the rhythm.

**Example 54: shuffle drum part**

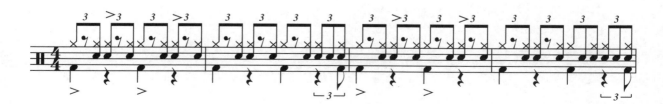

The typical shuffle bass line is based on the 6th chord – the 1st, 3rd, 5th, 6th and octave degrees of the scale, and the example here has a little rhythmic and melodic embellishment at the end of the bars. The bass rhythm uses each crotchet beat, which adds to the energy of this pattern and, with the drummer, really pushes the whole style along.

**Example 55: shuffle bass part**

The rhythm guitar will generally be a bright, thin electric guitar sound, to cut through the busy drums and bass lines. The 6/9 chords shown in Example 56 are traditional jazz harmonies and quite typical of the period, yet they add a uniqueness to the overall sound – it is hard to imagine a shuffle style without them. You can find out more about 6/9 chords and other chord substitutions in Chapter 2: Arranging.

**Example 56: shuffle guitar part**

The piano plays an important part in the shuffle style and, depending on the number of parts that your instrument's accompaniment style has, may be split over two parts – right and left hand. If you think of 'boogie-woogie', then you'll know exactly the feel that is required for this part, even if you don't recognise it in its written form. The right hand plays the third quaver triplet in each beat, which is in contrast to the left hand 'boogie' phrase. You'll certainly find this phrase somewhere in your shuffle or boogie accompaniments.

**Example 57: shuffle piano part**

The brass section is used mainly for punctuation in this style, and, as you can see in this example, it is adding octaves to the top note of the guitar part, using the same kind of phrasing. As most of the main work is done by the rhythm section, especially the piano, too much of anything else would just get in the way. Take note of the staccato accents on the short notes, which produce a good contrast to the softer, sustained notes.

**Example 58: shuffle brass part**

Another standard feature in popular music from this era is the 'close harmony' vocal backing group, and, as the modern voice sounds are now so good, this style gives the composer/arranger the ideal opportunity to feature them. Think of them as helping to support the main soloist: bars 1 and 3 provide a sustained chord, to give a sense of continuity whilst punctuated chords, similar to the brass and guitar, add contrast in bars 2 and 4. Use a vocal 'doo' sound for this 'close harmony' vocal part.

**Example 59: shuffle vocal 'doo' part**

The shuffle style is quite complex, so it is worth studying the following full score to see if you can identify the parts that might appear in any of your accompaniment styles. Listen to any style that uses terms such as shuffle, boogie or rock 'n' roll. Example 60 below shows all the shuffle parts in full score form.

**Example 60: shuffle full score**

53

## Beguine

Latin American styles are always a favourite, and none more so than the beguine. The drums and percussion have a gentle lilting quality which beautifully complements the orchestral rhythmic and sustained lines. The beguine is built on straight quaver beats, with syncopated and 'off' beat accents, which are easy on the ear and help create a moody and mellow performance. Normally played at around 120bpm, songs with longer notes and phrases work well in this style. In fact, most slower swing songs sound particularly pleasing when played against this easy Latin accompaniment.

There are many instrumental line-ups that can be used for the beguine and the example here is what you would typically expect to find on most instruments. So, as with previous examples, let's start with the drums.

**Example 61: beguine drum part**

*NB: The hi-hat in this style is played only with the pedal, as this gives a softer tone than playing with a stick.*

The Latin percussion includes congas, bongos and either claves or a cowbell (see Chapter 7: Instruments and Suggested Listening). The congas and bongos each come in two indefinite pitches (high and low) and are written as such – particular attention should be paid to the many accents falling on the second of the paired quaver notes.

**Example 62: beguine percussion part**

The easy-going nature of this style is reflected in the sustained notes and gentle rhythm of the bass line. As well as providing good support for the harmony, sustained bass notes help to create an unhurried and more flowing melodic performance, which is exactly the nature of this style. Notice how the bass drum plays a simple rhythm over the two bass guitar notes in bars 1 and 3 and how they both play a similar pattern in bars 2 and 4, except for the quaver note kick at the end of bar 4 (bass drum).

**Example 63: beguine bass part**

The sound of a nylon string acoustic guitar typifies one of the important rhythmic aspects of this style. The gentle strum of the first chord in bars 1 and 3 contrasts with the broken chords at beginning of bars 2 and 4. Given that this example (and all the other examples) is based on a chord of C major, you will notice that the chord in bars 2 and 4 is C6. Again, this is in keeping with the style, but it very much depends on the level of your instrument as to whether its accompaniment system can reproduce these chord extensions.

**Example 64: beguine guitar part**

Not everything in a Latin style needs to be percussive, and instruments that can play longer sustained notes are often used to create a stronger sense of tonality. The bass, although a percussive instrument (in as much as the initial pluck of the string is its loudest moment with the sound decaying from that point on) can, because of its longer strings, produce longer notes – as already seen in bars 1 and 3. This can be enhanced by the addition of a brass or woodwind section also playing the chords, and in this example, a soft brass ensemble duplicates the guitar's rhythm.

**Example 65: beguine brass part**

Although another percussive instrument, the marimba player uses a two-stick tremolo technique to alternate between different notes to create the illusion of sustained tones. Bars 1 and 3 show two whole notes – G and E – with a tremolo sign in between, and when heard, these notes will seem to be played together and last for four beats. Bars 2 and 4 not only have a similar device at beat four, using the notes E and G, but also the marimba has a little extra rhythmic phrasing of its own.

**Example 66: beguine marimba part**

A general wash of warm strings (pad sounds) will make a romantic style like the beguine sound complete. This could be achieved by using a string sound in your 'left part' – a part which plays to the left of your stereo area. However, many top of the range instruments are programmed to invert chords to their best sounding position within the accompaniment system, so it is quite common to have one of the accompaniment parts playing sustained pad chords as follows:

### Example 67: beguine string / pad part

The beguine is a fascinating style and is one of the easiest to play along with. Study the complete four bar score of what your instrument is likely to play, shown in Example 68 below.

### Example 68: beguine full score

## Concluding comments

Every manufacturer will offer unique intros, variations, fills and endings on their respective instruments, and it is probably these accompaniments that will influence your final choice when deciding which make and model to purchase. All of the examples in this chapter show what your instrument might do; they will at least be very similar, because all accompaniment styles are based on musical reality.

It should be remembered that all of these examples are based on what your accompaniment system will play when you play a basic triad chord of C major. Different chords will make the system play and add different notes, but that is the way your accompaniment feature is designed to work. Each manufacturer will have its own way of recognising and interpreting the chords that you play when the accompaniment system is working: it is not foolproof, but it should recognise most standard chords and a few more besides. The accompaniments are there to create good musical performances and to encourage you to play great music – whatever the style. Explore all that your accompaniment styles have to offer; learn from them, and, to a degree, be guided by them. They were written by professional musicians – so it is a bit like having a full time teacher by your side all the time.

## Composing your own styles

If your instrument has a feature that will let you compose your own accompaniment styles, then all of the score examples in this chapter can be used as a basic guide. You will have noticed that all the examples are based on four bar phrases. This is because 'middle of the road' pop music is generally structured on two, four, eight or twelve bar phrases or a multiple thereof. Therefore it makes sense that when composing your accompaniments you stay within these structured guidelines, and a four bar phrase is suitable for most combinations. You will also have noticed that the examples are all in the key of C major. The reason for this is that when programming your accompaniments, if you use any other key, then when you come to use them they will be 'out of key' with your melody; therefore it is vital that you compose all your accompaniments in C major.

The backing styles are a vital part of your instrument's music making capabilities: use them as you might use a real orchestra to accompany your melodic endeavours. It is not necessary to use all of the parts all of the time and their use does not constitute a lack of ability on your part if used well. After all, music is music no matter how it's made.

# 5. IMPROVISATION

Improvising can be described as instant melodic invention over a given chord sequence (harmonic progression), and may contain as many 'riffs', 'runs', 'licks', 'turns' and phrases as the performer can dream up. Improvising is an art, and as with all art forms can come quite naturally for some and not so for others. Although it is a natural ability for most jazz musicians, many of the basic ideas can be learned and incorporated into a creative arrangement at any grade. This chapter will also help when preparing for your Chord Sequence Test.

Improvising or extemporising is not a recent 20th century invention by jazz musicians. Improvising started as early as the 12th century with the art of vocal descants. In the 18th century, Handel and his contemporaries left the 'filling in' of the preludes to their keyboard suites entirely to the player, simply providing what we know today as a chord sequence from which the player had to develop the melody. Cadenzas in concertos are also a form of improvisation, in which Mozart, Beethoven and Liszt were so fertile in ideas.

It is often said (by people who are not fortunate enough to have had any musical training) that when they hear someone improvising – such as a trad jazz soloist or an Oscar Peterson piano solo – that what the performer is playing bears no relationship to the actual tune they started playing. However, if they were to sing the melody at the same time (assuming that they start in the right place of course) then everything would miraculously fall into place. This might be a simplistic scenario but in most cases, that is exactly how improvising works – using the same chord sequence (harmonic progression) and improvising, inventing or creating a new melody over it.

But why would you want to improvise? There are three main reasons:

- It adds interest for the listener, and of course the player;
- It will give your piece extra colour and texture, as developing the melody or chord sequence of a piece is far more musical than just repeating the tune;
- It will improve your knowledge of harmony, scales and rhythm.

In this chapter you will learn some ideas that will help you to understand the basic rudiments of improvisation; ideas that you can incorporate into any kind of music, particularly the pieces that you are already familiar with, and also utilising some of the general rules of harmony that you probably already know.

Adding a few embellishments to a piece may gain you a few extra exam marks, but more importantly, it will extend your own knowledge of how music works. It will also make your performances unique, and yet all of this can be accomplished with a minimum of understanding.

There are three main categories of improvisation:

- Rhythmic: Changing just the rhythm or time signature (the number of beats per bar);
- Melodic:    Playing a new melody based on the existing one;
- Harmonic: Playing rhythmic phrases using the existing chord notes plus any extensions or substitutions.

## Rhythmic improvisation

Here are the ascending and descending notes of the C major scale:

### Example 69

Keeping the crotchet note value and adding a 4/4 time signature, the scale will look like this:

### Example 70

You can see that the final C needs to be a minim in order to make up the correct number of beats in the bar. This extra beat could also be put at the beginning, like this:

### Example 71

The result here is that you have changed the way the scale feels when you play it, and it is likely that you will put the emphasis on the longer notes. Add an accent (>) on the first beat of each bar and the difference between the two versions will be even more pronounced:

### Example 72

As you can hear, a simple change in note length or accent can have a profound effect on the overall spirit of a piece.

The following example continues to use the same notes and time signature, but by simply altering the note values, some dramatic changes can be made:

**Example 73**

You can now apply this to your piece. The differences need not be great; shorten some notes and lengthen others – the most important thing is to create something that feels right to you.

Here are eleven bars of 'Lazy Afternoon' from the LCM Grade 4 keyboard handbook (LL175). Use an *Electric Guitar* sound for the melody with an 8-beat accompaniment style at around 90 bpm. Try to play the rhythm as written.

**Example 74**

Now try this:

**Example 75**

The spirit of the song has changed; you should now hear that the song is lighter and less formal. It still retains its eight beat format, and although some of the notes have been pushed nearer to each other in some cases – the dotted quaver/semi-quaver figures in bars 1, 5 and 8 for example – there seems to be a new brightness to the melody. This version of the melody might be appropriate at around Grade 5 level.

If you want the song to be in a swing style you can achieve this by making the quavers into 'rolling eighths', which means making the first one longer and the second one shorter. This sounds like (i), but can also be notated as in (ii) and (iii):

**Example 76**

Example 77 (on page 62) shows the result if you apply this to 'Lazy Afternoon'. Choose an Easy Swing accompaniment style at a moderate tempo – use just the drums, bass and strumming guitar part – and a tenor sax for the melody. You will also notice that some of the chords have been extended. Sixths are a characteristic of the swing/dance band style (see Chapter 2: Arranging). This version of the melody might be appropriate at around Grade 4 level.

**Example 77**

You can even play this song as a waltz – in three time instead of four. Played at around 85 bpm, it sounds light and playful. A Country Waltz accompaniment style would be good for this. This version of the melody might be appropriate at around Grade 5 level:

**Example 78**

If you keep the tempo the same and increase the note lengths, you will get a much more romantic and lilting waltz. There's also the opportunity to include more of the original chords too. Try Example 79 (on page 63) with an English or Viennese accompaniment style. This version of the melody might be appropriate at around Grade 4/5 level.

You could even try the additional versions shown in Examples 80 and 81. The version shown in Example 80 might be appropriate at around Grade 7 level; the version in Example 81 at about Grade 4/5.

You should be able to see by now that changing the rhythm of a melody can have a great impact on its perceived style. It is also a way of creating a melody that suits your own playing style: if you like to play swing, try playing an 8-beat pop song and change the quavers to 'rolling eighths' as in Example 77. If you prefer pop ballads, do the opposite – play 'straight eighths' instead and remove the 6th extensions in the chord progressions.

**Example 79**

**Example 80**

**Example 81**

## Melodic improvisation

Melodic improvisation keeps its roots firmly in the existing melody or melodic idea. It tends to be quite lyrical – more like a melody in its own right, and uses passing notes and non-chord tones to enhance the melodic interest. The aim here is to maintain the essence of the original melody yet adding musical ideas and phrases that are yours.

Here is a simple example:

**Example 82**

If you play it through a couple of times you will hear that really it is just a scale of C major with the addition of a few passing notes and a resolving 'one up' or 'one down' device at the end of each phrase. The point is that it sounds a little different – the melody has a few of *your* notes in it; you should also hear whether the added notes work or not, because your aural awareness should tell you. Passing chromatic notes are one way to bridge gaps between notes that are close together. When you get to the end of a phrase, play a note that is one note higher or lower than your final note so that you can move up to or drop down onto it. In Example 82 above, we drop down to the C in bar 2 and step up to the final note.

'Turns' using either the notes in the scale (diatonic) or chromatic notes are also useful for linking adjacent notes:

**Example 83**

Chromatic

(iii)

(iv)

And when they are incorporated into 'Lazy Afternoon' you can achieve some very pleasing effects, especially if you combine elements of melodic and rhythmic improvisation:

**Example 84**

| | |
|---|---|
| * | = Diatonic |
| ** | = Chromatic |
| *** | = Step up |
| **** | = Step down |

This version of the melody might be appropriate at Grade 6/7 level.

There are lots of other 'ornaments' – otherwise known as 'twists and turns'– that can also be very effective in adding interest to your piece. Once you begin to build up a library of your own favourites you will find that they can be added almost anywhere. Remember that all of this should be melodic, and although the underlying harmony needs to be taken into account, the emphasis is on developing the melody rather than on a complete extemporisation which only bears relation to the harmonic structure.

Example 85 shows some more ideas for you to try, and in a variety of common keys, so that you can see how they work. All of these patterns will prove valuable if you practise them carefully and with the correct fingering. Your teacher will be able to help with this.

**Example 85**

Sound used: Flugelhorn

Sound used: Clarinet

Sound used: Guitar

(iv)

Sound used: Vibraphone

(v)

Sound used: Accordion

(vi)

Sound used: Organ

**(vii)**

Sound used: Flute

**(viii)**

Sound used: Bassoon

**(ix)**

Sound used: Xylophone

Grace notes, such as acciaccaturas, are another means of ornamenting the melody. They are very short and only have a marginal time value: play them as if you had just caught a note by accident on the way to another note, giving them very little time value. These examples will show you how they work, and with time and practice you will be able to add many more of your own.

**Example 86**

Incorporated into 'Lazy Afternoon', the various melodic figures will produce the version shown in Example 87 below, which might be appropriate at Grade 7/8 level.

**Example 87**

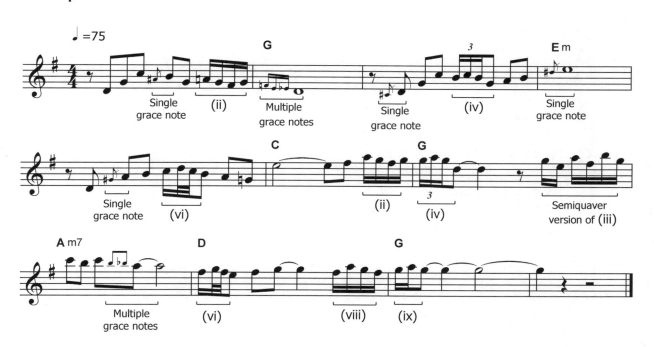

*NB: The bracketed numbers refer to patterns shown in Example 85.*

These are just a few ideas to give you an indication of how you might attempt some basic melodic improvisation. You will become more familiar with how these different phrases work and more importantly how they sound, and this will make it much easier to incorporate them into a piece. Furthermore, if you listen to music that features improvisation, you will hear many of the above examples, and begin to understand how they fit and what their effect is within a piece.

## Harmonic improvisation

In this approach to improvisation, the improvised melodic line is based on the supporting chord sequence (harmonic progression) rather than the existing melody. Not only does this give you the freedom to express your own musical ideas within a given harmonic framework, but also, to use it successfully you need to thoroughly understand how chords are constructed. Many keyboard players and organists may have learned their chord symbols by rote, rather than learning the basic theory behind a chord's composition. They will know each chord as a block of notes, rather than knowing the relevance of each individual note and its relationship to the other notes in the chord. However, you can still make an attempt at harmonic improvisation by working with the notes that you know.

It is not the intention here to cover this vast subject in great detail, but this section will give you sufficient improvisation skills for pieces that ask for an 'ad-lib solo'. This is only likely to appear as a requirement at Grade 8, however it is possible to use these techniques at any grade, providing the result is musical.

A simple explanation of harmonic improvisation is 'to instantly compose a new melody over an existing chord sequence' – the requirement needed for the Chord Sequence Test. This, if you know your chords, is not as difficult as it sounds, because if you play your chord notes individually, from bottom to top, then not only will you have a new tune, but it will also fit the chord sequence.

Example 88 shows the individual chord notes in crotchets and quavers, mainly ascending. Try playing this with a slow 8-beat accompaniment style and an electric piano voice with sustain.

**Example 88**

The result is not very imaginative or musical but it satisfies the brief. If you play the chord notes in both directions looking for sequential notes between chords, then you can achieve a much better musical result.

Try this:

**Example 89**

The crotchets in bars 3, 5, 7, 9 and 10 provide a good contrast to the constant rhythm of the quavers. Therefore, your new melodic line should be phrased with long and short notes just like any other melody; and as long as most of the notes are chord or scale tones, then pretty much anything goes. Here is an example for you to try that uses Example 89 but with some of the notes lengthened and some rests added:

**Example 90**

You can also use scales as the basic melodic material on which to base your improvisation. Use all of the notes in the major scale for major chords, and the same for 7th chords, but flatten the 7th note of the scale. This is known as the 'dominant seventh scale' or Mixolydian mode. For minor chords, use the notes in the 'natural' minor scale (Aeolian mode), and for minor 7th chords use the major scale but flatten the 3rd and 7th notes of the scale. This is known as the Dorian mode.

**Example 91**

...and even this can be turned into a professional sounding solo with just a little work on the note lengths. Try this (Example 92) as a saxophone solo with a slow 16-beat accompaniment style:

**Example 92**

You can produce even more notes to play around with if you add some chord substitutions and extensions (see Chapter 2: Arranging).

Try this smooth version of 'Lazy Afternoon' with a Romantic Swing accompaniment style at around 65 bpm and a deep tenor sax voice for the improvised melody. (If your instrument does not have a function that lets you nominate a different bass note for the chord, just play the chords as written and disregard the 'on-bass' notes.) The adaptation in Example 93 might be appropriate at Grade 8 / diploma level.

## Example 93

To enable you to experience other ideas for 'riffs' and phrases that can be played over a chord, Example 94 illustrates some helpful exercises on dominant 7ths and minor 7ths. These are basic ideas, in a variety of popular keys, which if practised often will be of great value. Listen as you play them, and try to remember the 'little tunes' that they create, because this way you will be able to remember them more easily.

The written notes are really chords and their numerous extensions in broken or arpeggiated form, and should be played over the given chord symbol; use them to build a library of improvised melodic lines that you can use with confidence to enhance your technique and performance skills.

## Example 94

Dominant 7th chords

## Minor 7th chords

Like any other art form, improvisation comes more easily to some than others, yet every aspiring musician can learn at least the basic essentials and explore the art of improvisation. The ability to hear the melodic and harmonic phrases that lie just beneath the surface of any piece will be rewarded tenfold, with a little effort.

### Further reading

| | |
|---|---|
| *Pentatonic Scales for the Jazz and Rock Keyboardist* by Jeff Burns | (Hal Leonard, 1997) |
| *Blues, Jazz and Rock Riffs for Keyboards* by William T. Eveleth | (Hal Leonard, 1993) |
| *Improvising Blues Piano* by Tim Richards | (Schott, 1997) |
| *Scales for Jazz Improvisation* by Dan Haerle | (Warner Bros., 1983) |
| *Exploring Jazz Scales for Keyboard* by Bill Boyd | (Hal Leonard, 1992) |
| *Jazz Piano Handbook 1* (LL184) | (LCM Publications, 2006) |
| *Jazz Piano Handbook 2* (LL185) | (LCM Publications, 2007) |
| *Popular Music Theory* grades 1-8 | (Registry Publications, 2001) |

# 6. AUTO-MELODIC HARMONY

This feature was originated by the Lowrey Organ Company in the USA back in the days when electronic organs were still valve-driven and long before computers and CPUs (central processing units) became the heart and brain of the modern instrument. 'AOC' or the Automatic Orchestra Control (later renamed the Automatic Organ Computer) as it was called, is a device that adds extra notes to a single-note melody. When the patent became public domain each manufacturer created their own terminology for the feature and extended the range of harmony types available.

'Technichord', 'Melody-on-chord', 'Auto Harmoniser', 'Harmony', 'Pro-Chord' and 'Music Assistant' are just a few of the names given to this feature by various manufacturers. Although you can, with practice, play some of these extra notes yourself, the accuracy and technical skill required to do this is something not usually attained for many years, and even then, the style of a manually played, fully chorded right hand melody is quite limited.

In this respect, it can be argued that even an experienced player will benefit by playing a single note melody and letting faster chorded phrases, or the more complex harmony notes – especially those which extend beyond the range of five right hand fingers – be played automatically by this feature.

The notes that your harmony feature adds are determined by the chord which is being played either on an organ's lower manual or to the left of a keyboard split point. These added notes, or a variation of them, are automatically transferred to the melody area and played below the melody note, using whatever melody registration is in use at the time.

There are many different variations for voicing instrumental sections of a band or orchestra, and most will be included in your 'harmony' feature with names such as 'close', 'open', 'duet', 'trio' 'block' and possibly 'full', 'brass', 'reed' and some kind of 'vocal' voicing. Although these terms might be unfamiliar to you, they are quite easy to understand and even easier to use.

Be aware that it is in the nature of this feature to add notes, so that a chord is heard; if you physically play groups of notes simultaneously at the lower end of your instrument, the resultant sound is likely to be an unpleasant and deep rumbling tone. Therefore, if you use your harmony feature and play low sounding notes, do not be surprised if it sounds unpleasant: a sound at concert pitch (8') will work well with 'harmony' from middle C upwards, while sounds voiced at 16' (an octave lower than concert pitch) are best played an octave higher.

To understand how this important feature works, here are some examples of different harmony and voicing types. They are based on a simple C major scale or broken chord.

### 'Basic' or 'Close' harmony

This will add the notes of the chord that is played in the left hand as closely as possible under the melody note. Example 95 shows a C major scale and an arpeggio over C and C6 chords for you to study. The played notes are solid and the automatically added notes are open.

**Example 95**

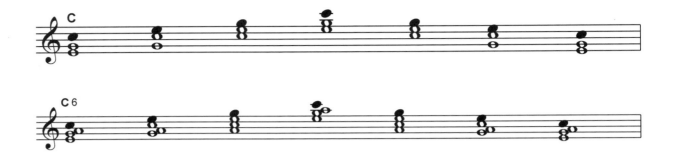

## Open harmony

In this style, the first note below the melody is transposed down one octave to give the chord a rich texture. This is a style that works well with strings and vocal sounds.

Here are two examples of a C major arpeggio, first over a basic C major chord and then a C6 chord:

**Example 96**

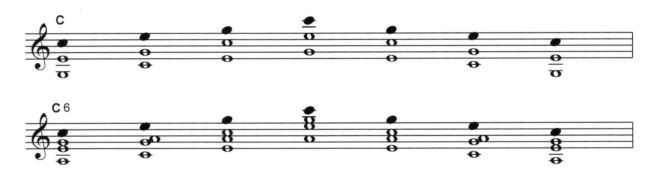

## Duet harmony

This is a variation of close harmony but, as its name implies, only adds one extra note to the played note, to produce a duet style. This works well with a trumpet for a Tijuana style or orchestrally with the horn. Duet harmony typically adds only the closest chord note, below the melody.

Here are two examples using a C major arpeggio over C and C6 chords:

**Example 97**

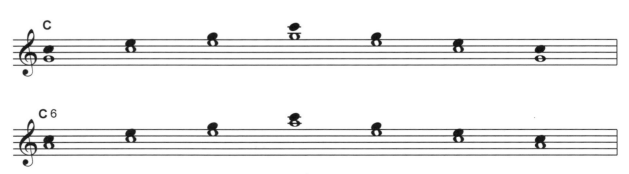

## Block harmony

Some of today's top of the range instruments will feature very stylised harmony types. For example, 'block' is based on the two-handed block chord piano style of George Shearing. For authenticity, this styling should contain a 6th in the harmony, together with major and minor 7ths, major 9ths and diminished chords for the non-chord notes in the melody. Additionally, the melody note is duplicated one octave lower. Your instrument's 'block' harmony will typically produce the following note additions to a C major scale and arpeggio:

**Example 98**

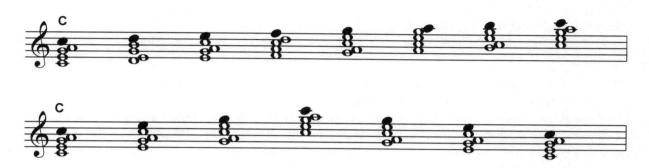

## Trio, Brass, Reeds & Choral harmony

This more advanced and intelligent harmony also has its derivatives, and these are detailed in the following examples. It is important to remember that, with the exception of 'vocal' harmony, which generally uses a four-part choral form, they are based on the '6th' style and are therefore more suited to swing and jazz idioms, rather than contemporary popular music.

**Example 99**

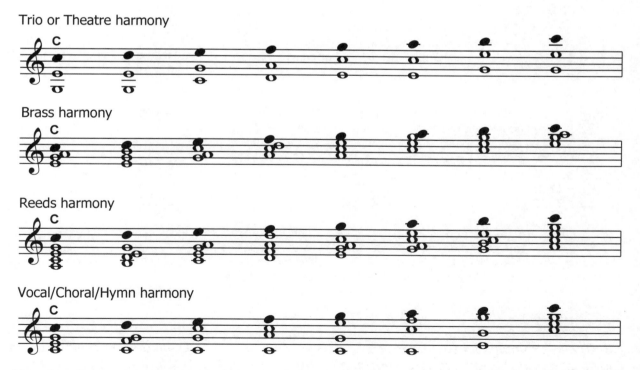

As with other features, every manufacturer will have its own version of auto-melodic harmony. Descriptive names such as 'trill' and 'octave' are common, as are '5ths', 'hard rock' (which work well with rock guitar sounds) and 'fanfare' for your brass sounds. All have their place in replicating harmony styles from group, band and orchestral sources.

## Auto-melodic harmony orchestration

On many of the mid to top range keyboards, the added notes that the 'harmony' feature produces can be assigned to different sections of the instrument. For example, assuming that your instrument lets you play at least two different right of split sounds simultaneously, one sound could be a solo instrument and the other a pad or supporting sound played in chords. Piano and strings, with piano being the lead sound supported by a harmonised string section is a favourite (Fig. 1), or maybe a solo trumpet with 'harmony' applied to an accompanying organ registration (Fig. 2). The more speaking parts your instrument has then the more musical possibilities are available., especially when using a 'full' harmony style (any which adds at least four notes).

The George Shearing sound for example, would feature vibes and jazz guitar playing an octave apart and a piano with 'block' harmony (Fig. 3) over a swing accompaniment style. Glenn Miller's reed section can be realised with a clarinet and a unison sax combination set an octave apart playing the melody with a soft alto sax sound with 'harmony' supplying the middle chords (Fig. 4).

Some instruments also feature multiple sound assignment where different added 'harmony' notes can be assigned a specific instrumental sound. Imagine the front line of a trad or dixieland jazz band – clarinet, trumpet and trombone. Using 'trio' harmony and multi-assign, the played note will have a clarinet sound, the first added note will sound only the trumpet, and the second added note will play with the trombone sound. Pan each of these sounds to the left, right and centre and using only the rhythm section from your Dixieland rhythm style, you'll have a really authentic sounding trad jazz set-up that imitates exactly what happens in reality (Fig. 5).

**Example 100**

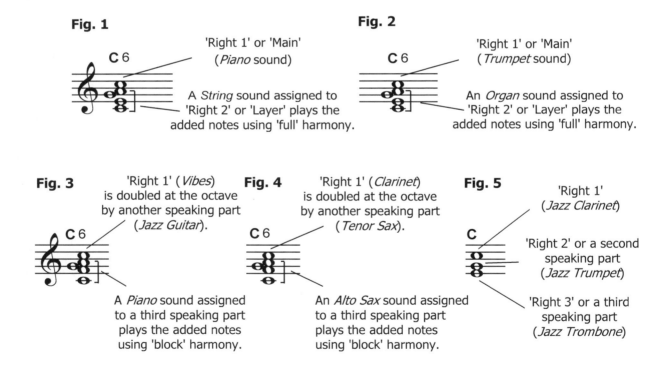

*NB: These examples illustrate what happens when you play a C melody note with a C or C6 chord, and use the auto-melodic harmony feature. The CD example plays each of the above setups as an arpeggio to enable you to hear the effect more clearly.*

To achieve creative and realistic arrangements, it is strongly recommended that you fully understand how this feature can musically enhance your performance skills.

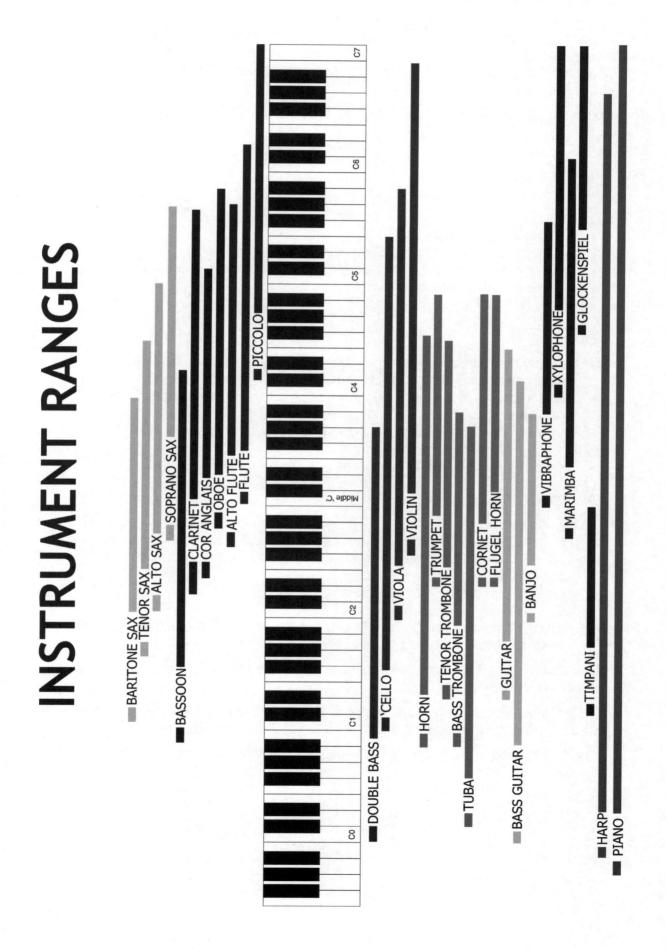

INSTRUMENT RANGES

# Woodwind Section

The term 'woodwind' can be misleading, as most of the instruments in this section are no longer made of wood any more. However, in their early stages of development, all but the saxophones used to be wooden. Flutes, for example, are now made from all kinds of metals including gold (James Galway – 'The Man with the Golden Flute') and the cheaper clarinets are made of plastic.

The woodwind section is made up from four different families – Flute, Oboe, Clarinet and Saxophone.

## Flute family

### Piccolo

- The smallest of the flute family.
- Like the flute, very agile with a very shrill tonal quality.
- Ideal for highlighting the melody in marches and dynamic classical passages.
- Not suited to solo passages, due to its piercing tone.
- Range: D4 to C7 (see range diagram)

### Flute

- Arguably the most agile member – which is why it is widely used in jazz and popular music as well as in classical music.
- Ideal for solo melodies as its bright tone can cut through most ensemble accompaniments.
- The most notable flautists in the popular and jazz music genre include Dave Valentin, James Galway and Philip Bent.
- Range: Middle C (C3) to D6 (see range diagram)

### Alto Flute

- A warm and mellow sound.
- Used frequently in film and TV music for its rich and melancholy tonal qualities.
- If your instrument does not have an alto flute sample, simply play the flute in its lower register to simulate this sound.
- Range: G2 to G5 (see range diagram)

There are various effects one can achieve from a flute and some manufacturers have been known to provide samples of these. The most common are:

- *Chiff Flute*: this effect is created when the player over-blows and gives the sound a percussive edge.

- *Flutter Flute*: flutter-tonguing is similar to the tremolo effect on strings. It is produced by a rapid fluttering of the tongue and is used to good effect in jazz improvisation passages.

- *Breathy Flute*: this effect highlights the player's breathy tone – especially effective in jazz playing.

## Oboe family

### Oboe

- A double reed instrument, probably the most lyrical of the woodwind family.
- Best range for a thin, softly piercing sound is between F4 and A5.
- Ideal for beautiful lyrical and melancholy melodies – 'love themes'.
- Range: Bb2 to A5 (see range diagram)

### Cor Anglais

- Sometimes known as the English horn.
- Larger than the oboe.
- A deep, rich and expressive tonal quality also suited to beautiful lyrical and melancholy melodies.
- Range: E2 to C5 (see range diagram)

### Bassoon

- The bass member of the woodwind section.
- A double reed instrument.
- Similar lyrical qualities to the oboe.
- A versatile and agile instrument suitable for dark and sombre melodies as well as lively staccato passages.
- Range: Bb0 to Eb4 (see range diagram)

## Clarinet

- A single reed instrument with a rich and mellow tone.
- Ideal for long sustained melodies and of course jazz standards.
- There are several types of clarinet (Bb, A, Eb and Bb bass clarinet), the most common being the Bb clarinet.
- The clarinet is a transposing instrument, which means a Bb clarinet sounds a major 2nd lower than what is written. This obviously does not apply to the clarinet sound, but it is useful to know in case you ever have to accompany a clarinettist. Other transposing instruments include the trumpet, cornet, flugelhorn, saxophone and French horn.
- Within popular music, the clarinet has been used as a featured solo instrument – the most notable examples of performers include Acker Bilk and Benny Goodman.
- Range: Bb Clarinet: E2 to A5 (see range diagram)

Like most instruments, the clarinet can produce various timbres. Most keyboards and organs provide a smooth classical timbre and a jazz timbre, which is slightly harsher with more attack to the note.

## Saxophone

The saxophone section is not a common component of a classical symphony orchestra although some classical composers have written for the various solo instruments (including Mussorgsky – *Pictures at an Exhibition*, Bizet – *L'Arlésienne*, Shostakovich – *Jazz Suites*), especially the Eb alto saxophone. In popular music the saxophone is much more common, either as a solo instrument or as a section in big bands and concert bands.

- Although made of brass, the saxophones are members of the woodwind family mainly because they are tonally closer to the clarinet family than to any other, and they are single reed instruments similar to the clarinet.
- Invented by Adolphe Sax around 1840.
- There are four types – Bb soprano, Eb alto, Bb tenor and Eb baritone.
- Commonly used in popular music genres such as big band, rhythm & blues and marching band for both ensemble and solo passages and as solo instruments in jazz and popular music.
- Within a big band the sax line-up would consist of two altos, two tenors and a baritone.
- Most modern saxophonists double on either flute or clarinet – sometimes both.
- The most famous sax soloists include Charlie Parker, Stan Getz, John Coltrane, Dexter Gordon, Sonny Rollins, Kenny G, Tom Scott, Michael Brecker, Benny Goodman and David Sanborn.
- Ranges: Bb Soprano – A2 to G5
         Eb Alto – Eb2 to Bb4
         Bb Tenor – A1 to G4
         Eb Baritone – Eb1 to Bb3
         (see range diagram)

# Brass Section

Originally, brass instruments were only used outdoors for hunting and military functions. Composers rarely composed for these instruments until they were fully developed around the 19th century. The early brass instruments sounded different and were quite difficult to play in tune with a good tone, making them very limiting. Possibly the only limitation today is the instruments' range, as brass players are among the most agile and versatile members of a symphony orchestra or band. Within a symphony orchestra you will find up to four horns, three trumpets, three trombones and a tuba. However, larger numbers of each can be found at times, especially for epic film soundtracks.

### Horn

- French horn is the traditional name, although today it is more commonly referred to as just 'horn'.
- Although a member of the brass section, the horn is sometimes seen as a member of the woodwind section, because of its ability to blend perfectly with, and strengthen, the woodwind ensemble.

- Played with a funnel-shaped mouthpiece, the horn has a conical bore with three valves.
- Mellower in tone than a trumpet, but has enough brilliance to cut through in louder passages.
- Ideal for both solo melodies and as a binding agent when accompanying.
- Used frequently in most genres from classical music to blockbuster movie scores, e.g. John Williams, Alan Silvestri, Danny Elfman, Howard Shore, James Newton Howard, Hans Zimmer.
- The horn is a transposing instrument in F, therefore sounds a fifth lower than written.
- Range: B0 to F4 (see range diagram)

Manufacturers offer various samples of horn effects, the most common being:

- *Muted Horn* – when a player puts a mute into the bell creating a softer tone.
- *Stopped Horn* – when the player inserts his/her hand in to the bell of the instrument. This creates a softer, smoother, nasal sound. Some manufacturers refer to this as *Closed Horn* (as opposed to *Open Horn*).

## Trumpet

- The most agile member of the brass section.
  - Its mid range gives a clear and bright sound while its upper register can be quite brilliant in tone.
    - Played with a cup mouthpiece, the trumpet has a conical bore with three valves.
      - There are several trumpets (Bb, C and D), the most common being the Bb trumpet.
        - There is also a piccolo trumpet, but this is only used in specialised music, such as music from the Baroque period.
          - Used frequently in all music genres from classical to pop, both in a section and as a soloist.
            - Within a symphony orchestra you would find three trumpets and in a big band you would normally find four.
              - The most notable soloists include Maynard Ferguson, Miles Davis, Chris Botti, Harry James, Dizzy Gillespie, Louis Armstrong, Wynton Marsalis and Arturo Sandoval.
                - Like the clarinet, the trumpet is a transposing instrument in Bb.
              - Range: Eb2 to Bb4 (see range diagram)

The trumpet is another instrument that has the facility to create different effects by using mutes, and again most manufacturers offer samples of these. The most common are the straight and Harmon cup mutes. The straight mute is commonly used in classical music and can be played softly or loudly. The Harmon mute is more commonly used in jazz idioms or for comical effects in light music. The sound of the Harmon mute gives a shimmering effect.

## Cornet

- Most commonly found in military bands or particular brass bands, where the cornet plays a similar role to that of the violin section within a symphony orchestra.
- Smaller in size than a trumpet, but with the same pitch range.
- A mellower tone than the trumpet.
- The cornet is played using a cup mouthpiece. Its bore is two-thirds conical and one third cylindrical and it has three valves.
- Ideal for melancholy lyrical melodies.
- Like the trumpet, the cornet is a transposing instrument in Bb.
- The most notable exponent of the cornet is Phillip McCann.
- Range: Eb2 to Bb4 (see range diagram)

### Flugelhorn

- The flugelhorn is a descendant of the keyed bugle.
- First manufactured in Austria between 1820 and 1830.
- The only difference between a flugelhorn and cornet is the flugelhorn's larger bell.
- It has a very lush mellow tone.
- Commonly used as a solo instrument in all jazz idioms, especially modern big bands.
- Like the cornet, the flugelhorn is a transposing instrument in Bb.
- Range: Eb2 to Bb4 (see range diagram)

### Trombone

- An extremely versatile member of the brass section because it is ideal for solos as well as providing a warm rich harmonic accompaniment in an ensemble.
- A mellow tone and a large dynamic range.
- Played with a mouthpiece, the trombone is cylindrical for about two-thirds of its length and becomes conical towards the bell.
- Commonly found in all musical genres from classical to pop.
- There are three types of trombone – alto, tenor and bass, although the most common are tenor and bass.
- As an ensemble there are normally two tenors and a bass trombone within an orchestra. Big bands normally have three tenors and a bass.
- Range:  Tenor – E1 to F4
          Bass – Bb0 to Bb3 (see range diagram)

As with the trumpets and horns, the trombones can create various effects using mutes. The most common of these are the cup and bucket mutes. The cup mute produces a muffled and nasal sound while the bucket mute produces not only a softer sound but also a more velvety mellow sound. These effects are standard in big band writing and most keyboard manufacturers now provide these sounds.

One common trombone effect is of course the glissando, which is executed by using the slide and portamento on keyboards and organs where possible.

### Tuba

- The real bass member of the brass section.
- Blends well with the trombones, trumpets and horns, providing an excellent bass.
- The most common use would be on the pedals of an organ when creating music in the marching/military band genre.
- Within a symphony orchestra you would normally find one tuba. It features occasionally in modern big band line-ups.
- Range: D0 to G3 (see range diagram)

## String Section

The members of the string section were the first instruments to be fully exploited by classical composers, and as a result, they became the main section within the symphony orchestra.

The reasons for this are:

- The string section was the first family of instruments to be technically fully developed – around 1700.
- From double bass to violin they encompass a massive range.
- They have a wide dynamic range as well as a variety of tone colours – pizzicato, marcato, tremolo.
- Unlike the woodwind and brass sections, the strings can play continuously without the player needing a rest in order to breathe.

## Violin

- The soprano member of the string section.
- Because of its many colouristic effects, the solo violin is probably the most difficult sound to sample, and therefore the sounds that are generally available are, on the whole, unconvincing.
- Played placed on the left shoulder, supported by the left side of the chin and held with the left arm and hand. Normally played with a bow.
- The *Fast Attack* sound (jazz violin) can be very effective for jazz or folk music.
- Notable exponents of the violin include, in the classical field, Yehudi Menuhin, Jascha Heifetz, Fritz Kreisler, Isaac Stern and Nigel Kennedy, and in the popular music field, Stephane Grappelli and Vanessa Mae.
  - Range: G2 to B6 (see range diagram)

### Viola

- The alto member of the string section.
- Slightly bigger in size than a violin with a beautiful dark-hued tone quality.
- Played like the violin, normally with a bow.
- Although in classical music there are a number of concertos written for the viola, it is generally used as an ensemble instrument.
- Range: C2 to A5 (see range diagram)

## Cello

- The tenor and, at times, the bass member of the string section.
- A rich and warm tonal quality.
- An ideal sound for enhancing counter-melodies, especially when doubled with the horns or clarinets.
- Like the viola, there are a number of concertos written for the cello, but in general the cello is used as an ensemble instrument.
- Range: C1 to E5 (see range diagram)

## Double Bass

- The real bass member of the string section.
- The only member that can have five strings, by adding a low C string by means of a mechanical extension.
- Normally played with a bow (*Bowed Bass*) but in popular music and especially jazz, the instrument is plucked – pizzicato (*Acoustic Bass*). This effect gives the sound more attack and provides the ideal drive for the rhythm section.
- Range: C0 to G3 (see range diagram)

The string section, like the woodwind and brass, also uses special effects. Generally the sounds that are commonly available include *Tremolo Strings* and *Pizzicato Strings.*

- The tremolo effect is created by bowing as quickly as possible during the length of the written note. This effect is very atmospheric and can be quite dramatic.
- Pizzicato is created when the player plucks the string as opposed to using a bow. This gives a very percussive attack to the note, and is used frequently in orchestral music of all genres.

### Harp

The harp is included here in the string section, because it is a stringed instrument and does not belong in the rhythm section alongside the other stringed instruments such as the guitars.

- The harp is probably one of the oldest instruments in the modern orchestra. Over the years the harp has seen many developments, resulting in today's double-action harp, which was finally developed during the late 18th and early 19th centuries.
- It has 47 strings and a range covering six octaves.
- Ideal for arpeggiated accompaniments during slow ballads, as well as crescendo glissandos during and at the end of dramatic pieces such as epic movie themes, power ballads, etc.
- Range: C0 to G6 (see range diagram)

### Harpsichord

The harpsichord, although it has a keyboard, is a member of the string family as its strings are plucked mechanically, unlike a piano whose strings are struck with hammers.

- It was developed during the 15th century predominantly in Italy and was the predecessor to the pianoforte. It has a bright and quite brittle sound and is frequently heard in music from the baroque period as both a solo and accompanying instrument.
- It is used today in popular music to create an 'antique' ambience – e.g. theme to the TV programmes 'Lovejoy' and the early 'Black Adder' series.
- The earliest example (c. 1521) can be seen in the Victoria and Albert Museum, London.
- Range: C1 toF5

# Rhythm Section

The rhythm section, as the name implies, provides not only the rhythmic foundation but also the basic harmonic foundation to any arrangement. Without this solid, tight rhythm section an arrangement can easily fall apart and become unmusical. Therefore, it is imperative that you spend time practising this section (left hand and auto accompaniment or left hand and pedals) separately, in order to achieve a strong foundation.

The instruments that make up a rhythm section can be quite diverse, but a basic section would comprise piano, guitar, bass guitar and drums.

## Acoustic Piano

- Various sounds are available ranging from a *Steinway Concert Grand* to a *Yamaha Upright* – each manufacturer has their own preferences. There are also 'MIDI Grands' available today; these are acoustic grand pianos with MIDI technology built in, so that the player can mix electronic samples together with the acoustic sound.
- Most manufacturers now include the harmonic acoustics and hammer noise in their piano samples, making this probably the most realistic of all the sounds.
- Mastering touch sensitivity and a pianistic left hand is vital when using this sound.
- Very much a solo instrument, but within a rhythm section, the piano helps to provide the harmonic and rhythmic foundation, especially in the absence of a rhythm guitar.
- In jazz and popular music the most famous pianists include Oscar Peterson, Count Basie, Bill Evans, Fats Waller, George Shearing, David Foster and Dave Grusin.
- Range: A00 to C7

## Electric Piano

The electric piano evolved as electronic engineers tried to create a piano sound, but in a package small enough to be transported from gig to gig. In 1962 the German company Hohner released an instrument called a Pianet which had a much smaller range than an acoustic piano, and the strings were replaced with tines or tone bars. This made a bell-like sound similar to a toy piano, but it was American pianist Harold Rhodes who really made a big impression with his Suitcase Rhodes Piano in 1965, although this had been in development since 1942. It was a self-amplified electric piano, again using tines instead of strings. It was called a suitcase piano, because it literally came in a suitcase, and the more modern versions are still being used today.

American jazz keyboard player George Duke, talking about the electric piano, said;

> The Rhodes electric piano could arguably be the most important instrument to come along in the 20th century. Before the synthesizer was actually available and became an active member of the music world, the Rhodes had become a standard in jazz, pop, rock and R&B.

In popular music the electric piano sound is therefore quite common. The most common of these are the *Modern EP* (a digital version of the suitcase) and of course the *Suitcase Piano*. Both have different qualities. The *Modern EP* produces a rich, warm sound ideal for those modern lush ballads, while the *Suitcase Piano* has more attack to the sound, making it more suited to jazz or more up-tempo pieces.

- Listen carefully to the type of instrument being used for the different musical styles, before deciding upon your choice of electric piano.
- Range: E0 to E6 (see range diagram)

**Guitar**

- Like the piano there are various sounds available, ranging from *Distortion Guitar* through to *Spanish Classical*. However, basically there are two generic types – acoustic and electric.
- The acoustic sounds are samples of acoustic guitars with either nylon strings or steel strings, as would be found on an electric or a 12-string guitar.

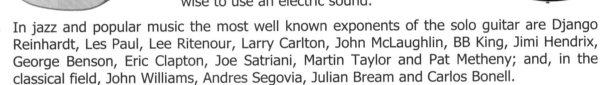

  - The electric sounds are samples of electric guitars with or without effects such as distortion, flange, phaser and chorus.
  - The first electric guitar was introduced by Rickenbacker in 1931, with the now famous Gibson 'Les Paul' model appearing in 1952.
  - In a standard rhythm section you would use either a smooth *Jazz Guitar* sound for vamping those lush jazz chords, or maybe a *Nylon Acoustic* sound for arpeggiating the harmony in a slow modern ballad.
  - When using the guitar as a solo instrument, the choice of sounds is yours, but always remember to keep the essence of the piece in mind. For example, if the piece has a heavy metal flavour, do not use an acoustic sound; if it has a classical flavour, it is not wise to use an electric sound.

- In jazz and popular music the most well known exponents of the solo guitar are Django Reinhardt, Les Paul, Lee Ritenour, Larry Carlton, John McLaughlin, BB King, Jimi Hendrix, George Benson, Eric Clapton, Joe Satriani, Martin Taylor and Pat Metheny; and, in the classical field, John Williams, Andres Segovia, Julian Bream and Carlos Bonell.
- Range: E1 to E4 (see range diagram)

**Bass Guitar**

- Usually a bass guitar has four strings, but five and six string basses are becoming more popular. The first Fender Precision Bass (a classic model with bass players) was first introduced in 1951 with the Fender Jazz Bass appearing in 1960.
- Again there is a multitude of sounds available, from traditional sounds such as *Acoustic Bass*, to *Slap Bass* (a sample of a bass playing technique used in modern popular music).
- When choosing a bass sound, think of the musical genre you are trying to create. If it's 40s jazz for instance, the bass player wouldn't be playing an electric bass using a slap technique, and conversely if it's 80's funk, the bass player is unlikely to be using an acoustic bass.
- The bass player provides the foundation from which the harmonic structure of the piece is built.
- It is also vitally important that, rhythmically, the bass is in tight sync with the drums, particularly the bass or kick drum.
- Well known exponents of the bass guitar are Abe Laboriel, Jaco Pastorius, Jimmi Haslip, John Patitucci and John Clayton, to name but a few.
- Range: C0 to C4 (see range diagram)

## Banjo

The banjo is similar to the guitar, in that it has a resonating body with strings. Instead of the body being made of wood it is a metal hoop with skin or parchment stretched over it, not unlike a drum.

- There can be 4 to 9 strings (usually 5 or 6) which pass over a low bridge and are then stopped against a fretless or fretted fingerboard.
- Some banjos have 'gut' strings which are played with the finger-tips, while a wire-strung banjo is played with a plectrum.
- The banjo is said to have originated in Africa, and during the 18th century it became popular with the negro slaves in the southern states of America.
- In the 19th century it was the main accompaniment instrument of the negro spirituals, and in the early 20th century it became the main rhythm instrument in the traditional (trad) jazz bands of New Orleans.
- Trad jazz and dixieland bands use a tenor banjo, which has similar tuning to that of the violin.
- Range: C2 to A3

## Drum Kit

As with all the instruments in the rhythm section, there are various drum kit sounds available to suit all musical genres, from orchestral percussion to the most up-to-date sounds of today.

The concept of the drum is as old as mankind, with the first drums appearing as far back as 6000BC. However, the drum kit as we know it today originated from the marching and parade bands in New Orleans. It was found that one player could quite easily play more than one drum simultaneously and with the later addition of cymbals and tom toms the modern drum kit started to take shape around 1930. In the 60s rock drummers then began expanding the standard kit by adding extra toms and cymbals, as well as a second kick drum to increase speed. Electronic drums were then developed in order to provide the drummer with sounds that traditional drums were unable to produce, and were introduced by Simmons in 1982.

A modern standard drum kit consists of the following:
- **Snare Drum**
- **Tom Toms** – the number can vary from two to five. These range in pitch from high to low.
- **Kick Drum (Bass Drum)** – sometimes two with a special pedal.
- **Hi-Hat** – a matched pair of cymbals operated by the left foot.
- **Cymbals** – these differ in size and type, e.g. crash, splash, and ride. The ride cymbal is used as an alternative to the hi-hat – especially in swing music.

Around this time there was also another innovation that would eventually enable a new style of pop music to evolve. The Roland Corporation introduced two instruments in 1982, namely the TB303 (Transistor Bass) and the TR606 (Transistor Rhythm). The TB303 was a programmable bass unit designed to emulate a real bass player and the TR606 was a programmable rhythm unit designed to emulate a real drummer. In 1987, a DJ rejuvenated the TB303 along with the TR606, and Acid House was born. Samples of the sounds that these two machines produce are available on the majority of electronic keyboards and organs, especially the more programmable models.

When programming drums, the most important thing to remember is that a live drummer only has two arms and two legs. Therefore, ensure your drum track is physically possible to play as this will give the track that live feel. Resist the temptation to quantize the track too rigidly, as this will only make the track sound 'inhuman' and computerised.

Choose the kit that best suits the genre to be created. This can be done by listening carefully to recordings of similar musical genres.

Some of the most notable drummers include Gene Krupa, Harvey Mason, Jeff Hamilton, Buddy Rich, Jack Parnell, Nikko McBrain, Billy Cobham, Dave Weckl, Steve Gadd and Alex Acuna to name but just a few.

# Percussion Section

Apart from the drum kit there is a multitude of percussion instruments that are available in the rhythm section and these can be split into two groups – definite pitch and indefinite pitch (tuned and untuned). Here are a few of the more commonly available percussion sounds:

## Tuned Percussion

### Vibraphone

- A popular jazz solo instrument sometimes referred to as 'vibes'.
- Sometimes appears in the orchestra to create a different timbre such as playing sustained chords together with the string section.
- An American design loosely based on the glockenspiel and introduced around 1924.
- Played with mallets on metal bars with resonating tubes below and uses the same key layout as a keyboard.
- It has a warm individual sound created by the resonating tubes and tremolo device.
- Most notable exponents of the vibraphone are Lionel Hampton, Roy Ayers and Gary Burton.
- Range: C3 to F5 (see range diagram)

### Xylophone

- The xylophone is very similar to the vibraphone in looks and is played in exactly the same way.
- The difference is that the xylophone has wooden bars instead of metal and until recently it didn't have resonators below; these add body to the very brittle sound.
- Played with hard rubber or plastic mallets, but for louder passages hard wooden mallets are used.
- The xylophone is ideal for adding a sharp edge to melodies being played by other sounds, especially rapid passages and has very little sustaining power.
- Range: C4 to C7 (see range diagram)

## Marimba

- A descendant of the xylophone.
- The marimba's rosewood bars with resonators produce a mellower and deeper tone than the xylophone.
- Since around 1950 the marimba has been more used within the modern symphony orchestra.
- Played with soft rubber mallets as opposed to hard rubber or plastic like the xylophone.
- Range: A2 to C6 (see range diagram)

## Glockenspiel

- Consists of two rows of steel bars and like the marimba has a keyboard layout.
- The steel bars are mounted on a frame within a portable case.
- Played with a brass mallet as this gives the loudest results.
- The oldest of all the mallet instruments dating back to the 19th century.
- Range: G4 to C7 (see range diagram)

## Timpani

- The oldest percussion member of the orchestra.
- There are five timpani ranging from 21"-32" in diameter. Until the early 20th century, timps had to be tuned by controlling the tightness of the calfskin membrane. To change the tuning took quite some time and so composers were limited to certain pitches within a piece. However, today's timpani have a pedal mechanism which enables the pitch to be changed much more quickly and easily.
- During the Classical period (1750-1820) only two timpani were common in an orchestra (28" and 25"), their role being basically to strengthen the tonic and dominant notes during climactic phrases or cadences.
- Beethoven was the first composer to use the timpani as a solo instrument (Symphony No.9 – Scherzo), and it was Berlioz's use of more than one set of timpani which led to the instrument's greater use and helped expand the range from two timps to five.
- Played with various mallets, hard, medium and soft, each giving a different timbre.
- The timpani can play single notes, rolls and, by using the pedals, glissandos. They have become a very versatile instrument.
- Range: C1 to C3 (see range diagram)

**Untuned Percussion**

For use in orchestral music, film and TV, etc.:
**Bass Drum, Snare Drum, Crash Cymbals, Tambourine, Tubular Bells, Triangle**

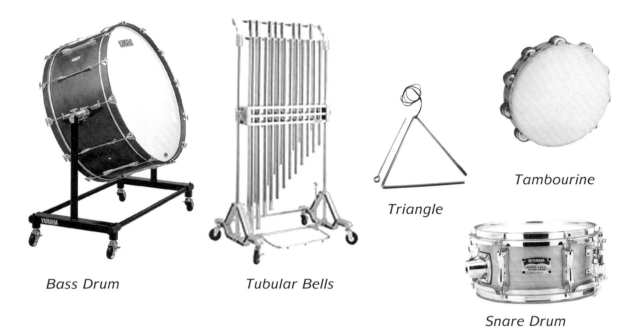

*Bass Drum*                *Tubular Bells*

*Triangle*

*Tambourine*

*Snare Drum*

For use in Latin music, popular music, etc.:
**Cabasa, Maracas, Tambourine, Claves, Timbales, Guiro, Cowbell, Congas, Bongos**.

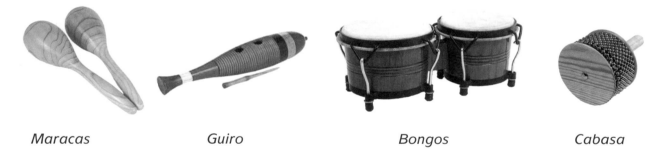

*Maracas*          *Guiro*              *Bongos*          *Cabasa*

# The Organ

The organ has been nicknamed 'The King of instruments' mainly because it has the largest pitch range of all the instruments in the orchestra. There are three types of organ sounds available:

- Pipe Organ or Classical Organ
- Theatre Organ
- Electronic Organ or Drawbar Organ

### Pipe Organ or Classical Organ

The organ can be traced back to the 10th century, and by the 17th century the organ had developed into something resembling today's instrument. The pedalboard was a German development during the 15th century, although it did not reach Britain until much later during the 17th century.

An organ consists of a series of pipes, graduated in size for pitch, which are fixed into a windchest fed by bellows. As the player depresses the keys, air is blown through the corresponding pipe and produces a sound.

There are two types of pipe – a flue and a reed pipe. The reed pipe has a vibrating tongue of metal which gives the sound a 'reedy' timbre, while the flue pipe, which is similar to a whistle, gives the sound a 'flutey' timbre. The various pipes are made of either wood or metal.

The normal pitch of an organ is an open-ended flue pipe – the 8' Open Diapason. Playing Middle C (C3), an 8' stop will pitch the same as a piano. A 4' stop will sound an octave higher and a 16' stop an octave lower. On the pedals you will also find a 32' stop – but you tend to feel this rather than hear it as it is so low in pitch!!

The keyboards on an organ are called manuals, and these vary in number. The largest instrument in the world has seven – Atlantic City Convention Hall, New Jersey, USA – although this is strictly a theatre organ. The largest classical organ was installed in Sydney Town Hall, Australia and was built by William Hill & Sons, London in 1890.

Generally there are three manuals:
- The lower manual, called the Choir Organ, is so named because the stops tend to produce a softer tone, and were initially used to accompany the choir.
- The middle manual is called the Great Organ. It has a variety of stops with a strong tone.
- The top manual is called the Swell Organ because all the stops are enclosed in a box with Venetian shutters which are controlled from the swell pedal, allowing subtle volume changes. If there is a fourth manual then this is normally referred to as the Solo Organ with stops of a 'solo' nature.

The pipe organ is not a common member of the orchestra as not all modern concert halls have one. However, there have been quite a number of concertos written for it over the past seventy years and its solo repertoire is extensive.

- Range: written C1 to C6, but by using a 32' stop and a 2' stop this can be increased either end by two octaves.


**Theatre Organ**

Between 1900 and 1930 a new art form took the world by storm – the movies – but in those days the cinema was not a multiplex as we know it today. Each town and city eventually boasted a large ornately decorated theatre which quickly became known as the 'movie palace'. These movies were not shown on small screens, but on big 'silver screens'. Everybody went to the movies, which at the time were silent, and normally, they would be part of a much bigger show.

The larger theatres employed musicians, in some cases complete orchestras, to accompany the stage acts, and although these shows were very popular, the impresarios who promoted them wanted something different, and the idea of installing a pipe organ in the auditorium was born.

Based on a traditional pipe organ, English inventor Robert Hope-Jones started to develop innovations that would eventually make the theatre organ capable of creating the sounds of an orchestra. As a result, it became a massive hit not only with the audience, but also with the impresarios, as it meant they could pay just one musician, as opposed to a full orchestra.

Robert Hope-Jones developed many of his innovations in England, but it wasn't until he visited America and forged a successful partnership with Rudolph Wurlitzer in New York that the 'Wurlitzer-Hope-Jones Unit Orchestra' was introduced. Almost overnight it became known as the 'Mighty Wurlitzer', but its official title truly reflected the instrument's nature: it had become a one-man substitute for an orchestra.

In 1927 the future of the theatre organ changed forever with the release of *The Jazz Singer*, a movie starring Al Jolson. The movie was the first of the 'talkies' and featured Al Jolson singing and speaking! Therefore, it was not long before the 'movie palaces' were installing speaker systems and as a consequence, the need for the theatre organ started to decline.

Today, due to the dedication and hard work of many enthusiasts, some of these fine theatre organs have been preserved, re-installed and modernised and can still be seen and heard in concert. Probably the most famous instrument in the UK is the Wurlitzer in Blackpool Tower.

## Electronic Organ or Drawbar Organ

The most famous electronic organ is the Hammond organ. Hammond, who also invented 3D glasses, was not a musician but a mechanical engineer. After leaving the Gray Motor Company in Detroit, where he was Chief Engineer, Hammond moved to New York where he developed the synchronous electric motor. He initially used this in the manufacture of electric clocks, but it ultimately led to the invention of the tone-wheel organ. His patent was filed on January 9th, 1934 and because of the widespread unemployment of the time (due to the depression), his patent was rushed through, in the hope it would create jobs for the area.

In 1935 the first Hammond Organ was introduced. It had two 61-note keyboards, a 25-note pedalboard and used external amplification, normally a rotary speaker.

The instrument used drawbars for each fundamental pitch – 16', 8', 4', 2', 1' together with the harmonics 5 1/3', 2 2/3', 1 3/5', and 1 1/3' etc. These drawbars are literally volume controls, giving the player an enormous amount of different tone colours.

In 1940 Don Leslie invented the Leslie speaker. This add-on rotary speaker literally throws the sound around the room creating the Doppler effect – like a police siren changing pitch as it moves towards you and then passes by. The sound is separated, with the high pitches being reproduced by a horn rotor and the low pitches by a bass rotor. Both can be operated at two speeds: fast (tremolo) and slow (chorale or chorus). Another effect is caused when switching from slow to fast. Because of the physical ballistics of the rotary mechanism, the speakers speed up or slow down when switched.

The early models also featured a traditional valve amplifier, which gave the sound a very 'warm tube' timbre. In modern instruments this 'sound effect' is digitally simulated.

In 1949 the first Spinet Organ was introduced – this had two 44 note keyboards and a 12 note pedalboard (no top C) with inbuilt amplification. The two best-known Hammond models were introduced in 1955 – the B3, favoured by jazz musicians, and the C3, favoured by many rock musicians. There have been many attempts to re-create the Hammond tone-wheel sound, but there is nothing quite like the original, even today – 70 years on.

Although used in all kinds of musical genres, the most famous use is in popular music, including rock but more particularly jazz. The most notable exponents of the Hammond included Booker T, Keith Emerson and Rick Wakeman, but the most famous jazz organist is Jimmy 'The Cat' Smith, who died aged 79, on February 8th, 2005.

## Pad Sounds

Pad sounds are a relatively new development. They are generally sounds taken from various classic synthesizers, both analogue and digital. A pad sound can take the place of any instrument that you could choose for sustaining the harmony within an arrangement. As most of the pad sounds available are of a contemporary nature, they can be quite limiting. However for modern ballads they can be very effective and offer a good alternative to the string ensemble. Each manufacturer has their own individual names for these sounds, but examples include: *Sweep Pad*, *Field of Voices*, *Warm String Pad*, *LA Piano Pad*.

## Other Sounds

The last two instruments are both members of the 'reed-organ' family and have a role to play in folk music, easy listening and popular music.

### Harmonica

The harmonica is the simplest example of an instrument that uses the 'Free Reed' principle (a reed which vibrates through an air slot, as opposed to against an air slot).

- It has a series of small metal reeds which are graduated in size. These reeds are enclosed in slots and encased in a short narrow box.
- Held against the lips and blown moving from side to side to achieve the desired note.
- Originated around the 1830s and also known as the mouth organ or blues harp.
- There are two types – diatonic and chromatic – which are available in different keys.
- The harmonica is a solo instrument suitable for jazz, 'middle of the road' and popular music melodies.
- The most famous virtuosos of the harmonica are jazz musicians Toots Thielemans and Larry Adler, and for pop music, Stevie Wonder.
- Range: C2 to D6 (chromatic – 64 reeds)

## Accordion

- In principle this instrument works in the same way as the harmonica; however, the notes are generated by bellows, not breath.
- Played with two hands, while squeezing the bellows in and out.
- The left hand uses a series of buttons which provide simple major, minor and diminished chords, while the right hand plays the melody, again using a series of studs or buttons.
- Piano accordions use the same system for producing the chords, with the right hand using a traditional three and a half octave keyboard for the melody.
- The more advanced accordions have stops or preset registrations which alter the tone of the instrument.

- The most popular use of the accordion is in folk music, especially German polka bands, and it is synonymous with French and Italian traditional music.
- The most famous virtuosi of the accordion are Jack Emblow, Marco Santori, Art Van Damme, and the legendary Scottish musician Jimmy Shand.
- Range: F2 to C5

We are grateful to the following parties for their permission to reprint copyright images in this publication:

Ross Mallets / Jupiter Band Instruments for the Vibraphone, Marimba, Xylophone and Glockenspiel;
Hobgoblin Music for the Banjo, Triangle, Tambourine, Bongos, Cabasa, Guiro, Maracas, Harmonica and Accordion;
Allen Organ Company for the Classical and Theatre Organ;
Buffet Crampon for the Cor Anglais and Bassoon;
Pilgrim Harps for the Harp;
www.hammondorgan.co.uk for the Hammond Organ and Leslie Speaker;
www.earlymusicshop.com for the Harpsichord;
Yamaha Kemble Music for pictures from the Yamaha Picture Archive

# SUGGESTED LISTENING

Listen to the recommended recordings to hear examples of the instruments and how they are used. The majority of these recordings are available worldwide from music shops or from on-line retailers such as Amazon and iTunes. Most of the artists have their own dedicated websites, so if you have difficulty locating any of these recordings, then use the individual websites to find further information about their availability.

## Flute
- James Galway: *Galway at the Movies*
- Dave Valentin: *World on a String*

## Oboe
- Ennio Morricone: 'Gabriel's Oboe' from *The Mission*

## Bassoon
- Grieg: 'In the Hall of the Mountain King' from *Peer Gynt Suite*
- Stravinsky: *The Rite of Spring* (opening)

## Clarinet
- Acker Bilk: *The Frankfurt Concert 1966*
- Eddie Daniels: *This is Now*
- Benny Goodman: *Benny Goodman*

## Saxophone
- Charlie Parker: *Ultimate Charlie Parker*
- Any Dexter Gordon / John Coltrane recording
- Kenny G: *Classics in the Key of G*
- Tubby Hayes: *Tubbs*
- Stan Getz: *Getz / Gilberto Vol. 1*
- Johnny Dankworth / Cleo Laine: *Collection*
- Paul Desmond: *Feeling Blue*
- Charlie Parker: *Yardbird Suite*
- John Coltrane: *A Love Supreme*
- David Sanborn: *Closer*
- Dave Koz: *At the Movies*
- Tom Scott: *Them Changes*
- Walter Beasley: *For Your Pleasure*

**Useful websites**

www.virginmegastores.co.uk – general music
www.towerrecords.com – general music
www.martinrecords.com – theatre organ
www.worldmilitarybands.com – military bands
www.discurio.com – military bands, choir and organ
www.counterpoint-music.com – jazz
www.jazzloft.com – jazz
www.smoothtrax.com – jazz
www.soulbrother.com – jazz
www.silverdisc.com – easy listening
www.bigbandcdstore.com – big band
www.ukcd.net – brass and military band

## Trumpet
- Dizzy Gillespie: *Dizzy for President*
- Miles Davis: *Ballads and Blues*
- Arturo Sandoval: *I Remember Clifford*
- Eddie Calvert: *The Very Best of Eddie Calvert*
- Maynard Ferguson: *The Essential Maynard Ferguson*
- Rick Braun: *Kisses in the Rain*
- Alison Balsom: *Bach – Trumpet & Organ Recital*
- Chris Botti: *To Love Again*
- Louis Armstrong: *The Definitive Collection*

## Cornet
- Wynton Marsalis: *Carnaval*
- Phillip McCann: *All of the World's Beautiful Melodies – The Golden Cornet of Phillip McCann*

## Trombone
- Don Lusher / Maurice Murphy: *Just Good Friends*
- John Allred: *Focused*
- Mark Nightingale: *Destiny*

## Violin
- Vanessa Mae: *The Violin Player*
- Stephane Grappelli / Yehudi Menuhin: *The Very Best of Grappelli and Menuhin*
- Joshua Bell: *The Essential Joshua Bell*
- Nigel Kennedy: *Vivaldi – The Four Seasons, Blue Note Sessions*

## Cello

- Julian Lloyd Webber: *Made in England*
- Yo-Yo Ma: *Yo-Yo Ma Plays the Music of John Williams*
- Yo-Yo Ma / Stephane Grappelli: *Anything Goes*
- Berlin Philharmonic Cellists: *Beatles in Classics*

## Harp

- Roberto Perera: *In the Mood*
- Catrin Finch: *String Theory*

## Acoustic Piano

- William Joseph: *Within*
- Keiko Matsui: *The Piano*
- Dave Grusin: *Now Playing – Movie Themes*
- Oscar Peterson: *Plays the Duke Ellington Songbook*
- Monty Alexander: *Live at the Iridium*
- Laurie Holloway: *The Piano Player*
- Dick Hyman: *The Honky-Tonk Professor*
- George Shearing: *The Definitive George Shearing*
- Yanni: *Ultimate Yanni*
- David Foster: *The Symphony Sessions*
- Bobby Lyle: *The Power of Touch*
- Lyle Mays: *Lyle Mays*
- Ramsey Lewis: *Dance of The Soul*
- Joe Sample: *Ashes to Ashes*
- Jonathan Cain: *Piano with a View*

## Electric Piano

- The Crusaders: *Street Life*
- Stevie Wonder: *Talking Book*
- Donald Fagen: *The Nightfly*

## Acoustic / Semi-acoustic / Jazz Guitar

- Acoustic Alchemy: *The Beautiful Game*
- Peter White: *Perfect Moment*
- Martin Taylor: *Kiss and Tell*
- Django Reinhardt: *Guitar Genius*
- Earl Klugh: *Late Night Guitar*
- Joe Pass: *For Django*
- Antonio Carlos Jobim: *Wave*
- Wes Montgomery: *The Best of Wes Montgomery*

## Electric Guitar

- Lee Ritenour: *Collection*
- Pat Metheny: *We Live Here*
- George Benson: *The Best of George Benson*
- Joe Satriani: *Surfing with the Alien*
- Eric Clapton: *The Cream of Eric Clapton*
- Larry Carlton: *Fingerprints*
- Chuck Loeb: *Presence*
- Gary Moore: *Back on the Streets*

## Bass Guitar

- Niels Pedersen: *Kenny Drew & Niels-Henning Orsted Pedersen*
- Abe Laboriel: *Justo Almario & Abraham Laboriel*
- John Patitucci: *Heart of the Bass*
- Marcus Miller: *Live & More*
- Jimmy Haslip: *Red Heat*

### Drums
- Buddy Rich: *Live at Ronnie Scott's*
- Billy Cobham: *A Funky Thide of Sings*
- Dave Weckl: *Multiplicity*
- Gene Krupa & Louis Bellson: *The Mighty Two*
- Alex Acuna: *Acuarela de Tambores*
- Harvey Mason: *Groovin' You*
- Omar Hakim: *Rhythm Deep*

### Vibraphone
- Roy Ayers: *Live at Ronnie Scott's*
- Gary Burton: *Next Generation*
- Lionel Hampton: *There Will Never Be Another You*

### Percussion
- Paulinho da Costa: see www.paulinho.com
- Various Artists: *The Soul of Percussion*

### Classical Organ
- Marie-Claire Alain: *Great Toccatas*

### Theatre Organ
- Reginald Dixon: *Reginald Dixon at the Blackpool Tower*
- Phil Kelsall: *Love Changes Everything*
- Buddy Cole: *Hot and Cole*
- Jesse Crawford: *Melodies and Moods*
- George Wright: *Command Performance*
- Nigel Odgen: *From Stage & Screen*
- Brian Sharp: *From the Tower*

### Jazz (Hammond) Organ
- Jimmy Smith: *The Cat*
- James Taylor Quartet: *Room at the Top*
- Joey DeFrancesco: *Singin' and Swingin'*
- Mike Carr: *Stephenson's Rocket*
- Harry Stoneham: *Live at Abbey Road*

### Accordion
- Jack Emblow: *Enjoy Yourself*
- Art Van Damme: *Once Over / Manhattan Time*
- Jimmy Shand: *The Legendary Jimmy Shand*

### Harmonica
- Toots Thielemans: *Essential Toots Thielemans*
- Larry Adler: *The Great Larry Adler*


## Styles and larger groups of instruments

### Film Orchestra

There are many great film scores to listen to and learn from, in fact far too many to list individually. The list below represents a wide range of styles from the world's greatest film composers. For more information on film music, www.musicfromthemovies.com is very informative.

David Arnold, Craig Armstrong, John Barry, Elmer Bernstein, Klaus Badelt, Patrick Doyle, John Debney, Danny Elfman, George Fenton, Dave Grusin, Ron Goodwin, Jerry Goldsmith, Nigel Hess, James Horner, Maurice Jarre, Erich Korngold, Henry Mancini, Lalo Schifrin, Howard Shore, Alan Silvestri, John Williams, Harry Gregson Williams, Gabriel Yared, Hans Zimmer

## Big Band
- Stan Kenton: *The Best of Stan Kenton*
- Carl Saunders: *Be Bop Big Band*
- Quincy Jones: *Big Band Bossa Nova*
- GRP All-Star Big Band: *GRP All-Star Big Band Live*
- Big Phat Band: *Big Phat Band*
- The Phil Collins Big Band: *A Hot Night in Paris*
- Count Basie: *The Count Basie Story*
- Jools Holland & his Rhythm & Blues Orchestra: *Small World Big Band Vol. 1*
- Glenn Miller: *The Essential Glenn Miller*

## Brass Band
- The Black Dyke Mills Band: *The Essential Dyke*

## Full Orchestra
- Britten: *The Young Person's Guide to the Orchestra*
- Joni Mitchell, arr. Vince Mendoza: *Both Sides Now*
- Kenny Rogers, arr. David Foster: *Timepiece*
- David Foster: *Rechordings*
- Barbra Streisand, arr. Jeremy Lubbock / Jorge Calandrelli: *The Movie Album*
- James Last and his Orchestra: *Pop Symphonies 2*
- Paul Mauriat and his Orchestra: *Classics in the Air*
- Boston Pops Orchestra: Any recording, with either John Williams or Arthur Fiedler

## Light Music String Orchestra
- Diana Krall, arr. Claus Ogerman: *The Look of Love*
- Shirley Horn, arr. Johnny Mandel: *Here's to Life*
- George Benson, arr. Claus Ogerman: *Breezin'*

## Classical String Orchestra
- Barber: *Adagio for Strings*
- Vaughan Williams: *Fantasia on a Theme by Thomas Tallis*
- Holst: *St. Paul's Suite*
- Warlock: *Capriol Suite*

## Orchestral Wind Band / Marching Band
- The Regimental Band of the Coldstream Guards: *Marches 1 – British*
- The Regimental Band of the Coldstream Guards: *Guards in Concert*
- Martin Ellerby: *The Cries of London*

## Trad Jazz
- Kenny Ball: *Greatest Hits*
- Acker Bilk / Chris Barber / Kenny Ball: *Acker, Kenny and Chris*

## Music Theatre
- William David Brohn: Orchestration of *Mary Poppins / Miss Saigon*
- John Cameron: Orchestration of *Les Miserables*
- David Cullen: Orchestration of *The Phantom of the Opera*

## Improvisation
- Keith Jarrett: *Keith Jarrett Trio Concert 1996*
- Pat Metheny: *Imaginary Day, The Road to You, Secret Story (with the LSO)*
- Oscar Peterson: *The Genius of Oscar Peterson*
- Michel Petrucciani: *Playground, Both Worlds*
- Lyle Mays: *Improvisations for Expanded Piano*
- Bob James: *An Anthology*